A Bear
AND A
Dove

A Journey of Faith

Dove Morgan-Osborne

Loving Hearts
Ministry

Bristow, OK

A Bear and A Dove—A Journey of Faith
Published by:
Loving Hearts Ministry
P.O. Box 928, Bristow, OK 74010
ISBN 0-9789396-0-3
www.lovingheartsministry.org

Cover design and book production by:
Silver Lining Creative
www.silverliningcreative.com

Printed in the United States of America.

A Tribute

This book is a tribute to the goodness of God declaring that He is the same God for the wealthy as He is for the down and out. He is the same giver for the educated as He is for the illiterate. God is not a respecter of persons, but He is a respecter of faith. This book is a simple tribute to God's supernatural provision and those that the world said couldn't make it.

This Book belong to Elizabeth

Contents

Foreword

I am honored to stand with and share this awesome testimony of love, grace, and restoration from the heart and life of Dove Morgan-Osborne. You are going to be so blessed reading this true story of how when it seems people are finished with you, God is just getting started! Bear Morgan's life proves that God will always give you another chance, but that the choice is yours to take it — and when you do *He will restore all your depleted areas, placing His strength where your weakness was.*

When God joined Dove and Bear in their marital and ministerial covenant, through Him they were strategically positioned in exactly the right place, at the right time, to carry out the vision and the destiny He had for them.

And yes, in the beginning that 'right place' was a prison; and yes, that 'right time' included periods of homelessness, loss, lack, and attack by the enemy (sounds like the Apostle Paul in 2 Corinthians, 11:23-27!). But God knew to choose and use Bear to show the countless people whose lives he touched how, through God's grace, *we can be damaged, but still delivered;* and to call Dove to manifest the healing, transformational power of His unconditional and unfailing love. A true story of "nothing is impossible with God!"

In Dove and Bear, Jesus Christ found two warriors, who He perfectly equipped to deliver His message of *freedom and eternal life through Him;* they took His message beyond cultural and racial boundaries, beyond economic and class divisions, and beyond the conventional walls of any church. Whether they were on the backs of their Harleys, among the leathers and tattoos of those they touched, or in their own home, as they opened their arms to countless men traveling in and out of prison, they shared the love and grace of God through the destiny He chose for them.

You will discover that unconditional love, grace, and restoration, as you are inspired by their vulnerability and desire to openly expose a life transformed by God. I have been blessed to have been able to share time and fellowship with Dove and Bear for many years. They change you!

Dove and Bear's journey proves how God's provision, blessings and favor will make a way when there seems to be no way, when we proclaim His name and serve Him from where we are. Enjoy...be inspired... and always know — God takes what others see as "black coal" and polishes it, to bring forth the beautiful, strong, brilliant shining diamond! *Through Him, nothing is impossible!*

— Paula White
　　Without Walls International Church
　　Paula White Ministries
　　Tampa, Florida

Chapter 1
The Beginning

I waited patiently for the Lord; He inclined unto me, and heard my cry.

He brought me up also out of an horrible pit, out of the miry clay, and set my feet upon a rock, and established my goings.

Psalm 40:1,2

One and a half year old Richard with his mother.

Molested at age seven by a family member and threatened with his life not to tell, *Richard Lee Morgan* became filled with a near insane hatred and rage even as a young boy. He was frequently in trouble and constantly in and out of juvenile institutions. By the time he was 17, he was arrested and tried as an adult, convicted and sentenced, entering prison at age 18. Richard then became a part of some of the most horrible riots, killings and crime in the history of the United States prison system.

While Richard Morgan was 16 and heading to prison, I was a twelve year

Eight year old Richard.

old girl with an alcoholic father that was never home. I remember many times my mom would put us in an old pickup to go look for Dad. He would be drunk, but feel bad about his behavior. Several times I remember he was taking care of me when I was fairly little and hid me under the pool table at the bar. Dad was proud of me, his little "palomino filly," as he called me. Sometimes Dad would bring me home "goodies" from poker games that he won. I remember he proudly won a western shirt and had me put it on, even though it was at least six sizes too big. Finally, my mom had to do something about his lack of wisdom when he lost the family car in a poker game at the bar. A divorce was arranged before the family lost anything else.

Somehow as I witnessed what my Dad did and what my mom went through, as I got older it gave me a huge heart for those that were drug addicts, alcoholics, and those that were locked up. Even long before I knew the Lord, God was dealing with my heart to be a person that would reach out to those that society looked down on. Then as a senior in high school, a friend took me to a revival where I received Jesus Christ as my personal Savior. When I was 19, I was married and then had three wonderful sons, Riley, Ty and Lain. My husband and I grew apart through those years and looking back on it, I'm the one that gave up on the marriage. I would certainly handle things differently today than I did then. Thank God there is life after divorce.

In 1988, I started in prison ministry and a couple years later met Bear Morgan. He was in a correctional facility near Portland, Oregon, called Larch Mountain Corrections. He was soon to be transferred to Walla Walla, Washington, where he had done much of his hard time.

Chapter 2
My Man is a Prisoner

But God commended His love toward us, in that while we were yet sinners, Christ died for us.

Romans 5:8

When I met Bear, he had nearly a year left to do. Before he committed his life to Jesus Christ as Lord and Savior, he was known as *Mad Dog* Morgan, a man notorious for his uncommon brutality and the reputation of an outlaw. Several times he had a contract on his life. After having lived such a life filled with crime and hate, Bear asked Jesus Christ to become

his personal Lord and Savior in 1989 while attending a KAIROS Prison retreat in Monroe, Washington.

Nearly 300 pounds, 6' 3", and of Cherokee heritage, Mad Dog then became *Bear*. A Catholic nun spoke to Mad Dog after he received Jesus and told him he needed a name change. She said he was no longer a *mad dog*, but now was a gentle *Teddy Bear*. So the name *Bear* stuck. Bear committed to serve God for the rest of his life with all of his heart.

The first time I heard of Mad Dog Morgan, I was attending a volunteer workshop in Pendleton, Oregon. I sat as I listened to the leaders share why as a volunteer,

3

you never want to get close to an inmate. They were speaking of a prison called Walla Walla — that had a hallway called, *Blood Alley*, where blood was shed every week. They were sharing stories about the toughest of criminals and mentioned Mad Dog Morgan as being one of them. As I sat through that meeting, there was no way that I would have believed I would be married to that very man someday.

Bear and I met as I was going in to minister in several units. I was actually taking a lady in to see her husband and helping them to be reconciled. God joined Bear and I together and we knew we were destined to serve Him as a team in the free world.

One day while Bear was in prayer over us getting together, God spoke to him to call me *White Dove*. Bear was so excited that he had to call me and tell me right then.

"Guess what? I have a special name for you!"

"Really? What is it?" I sounded excited, but I was actually a little hesitant as I knew some of the stories Bear had told me of women that were named by their men. Names like "Godzilla" and "Beefer" came to mind when he said that he had a name for me. I was listening closely.

"The Lord told me today that you're my White Dove. You know the song, *On the Wings of a Snow White Dove* by Ferlin Huskey? Well, you were sent by God just like the song says. You're His sign from above." We also knew that with both of us having Cherokee backgrounds, *White Dove* just fit well.

It was truly a name from the Lord. As time passed, most of the time the name was shortened to *Dove* and that's what I've been going by ever since.

During our weekly visits at the prison, we knew God had a big call on our lives. Sometimes we would sit the entire time of our visit just talking about how we would have a ministry that would go around the world preaching the Good News of Jesus Christ. Long before Bear ever got out, we had a *worldwide ministry already birthed in our hearts.* We had big dreams, big desires and we knew we served a big God and that nothing was impossible through Him.

Bear and Dove at a prison visit.

Chapter 3
How Do You Say It?

It was hard having a loved one in prison and I really thought all of our problems would be over when Bear was released. Bear was trying to warn me as he shared a copy of this *Lonely Letter Home* with me in one of the cards he sent while he was still locked up in the early part of 1991.

The Lonely Letter Home....

How do you say it? (Will you really be ready for me when I get out?)

...How do you say it?...That which you want known to a special someone beyond the walls?...No one can ever know...No one who hasn't been a blue-clad, faceless numbered nothing. I can't tell them, but I can try...I'm going to be different when I get out...I'll never be the same...and I want someone to understand...

...Understand that if I feel hostile and defensive, it is because every facet of my gray world is a threat to the soft, mellow, secret things I keep inside me. I cannot trot out gentleness, because in my world nothing is gentle. I cannot show kindness, because kindness is a weakness in my world, and to be weak is to invite more hurt. I dare not exhibit love, because in my world, the bars and mocking locked doors would rip it to bloody shreds. I cannot bring forth and demonstrate my loneliness or hungers because they have become a bone-deep ache that can't be reached or soothed. You have to know....

...To know that while other young men my age grew up watching fat babies grow into healthy youngsters, I grew up watching healthy youngsters having their guts and minds twisted and ripped and being turned into emotional cripples. While the young men you knew were learning their trades, I was listening to the belches of 1,000 men in a human zoo. Don't pity me. I don't want your pity. Just understand me....

...Understand me and the way I changed inside when they stripped away my identity and self respect. Changed day after day by being treated like an idiot child and being forced to live with every type of human derelict. Changed by the indignity of being forced to scurry like a mindless fool every time a guard's voice barked or a bell rang. Never being able to escape the guard's uncaring or hostile eyes, living in a fish bowl, where you can't even squat on a toilet without an audience. Can you begin to see the shell forming, the first of many calloused layers of rigid resistance that serve as a protection for the human warmth and sensitivity necessary for sanity....

...Can you begin to see how being stripped naked and having the guards degrading fingers searching, probing my body, can leave wounds on pride and dignity that are a long time healing and leave ugly scars?...Can you understand that in the face of constant assault of personalities, I am forced to turn off my emotional faucet, dry up the full range of feelings for love, compassion, indignation, repugnance, or lose my mind? I survive by playing a role...acting out a part for indifferent eyes...hiding what I really am away from the contamination of this soul-sick world...I became tough, hardened, and cold because my world demands it. Tough, hardened and cold — until night comes...I lay there and think with my emotions boiling inside me...always inside. Inside where no one else can see...I ride on an emotional roller coaster...

...When I come out, can you accept the restlessness of a bird newly released from a cage? Accept my clumsiness until I learn how to act with real world people? Accept blunt honesty when I awkwardly try to reassure you?...Can you really know that I don't hear the drum beat to which most men march their lives?...That the master drummer of my destiny is as old as time and demands of me a more intricate step?...Can you know the kind of man I am down deep inside when the first steel gate slammed shut — separating me from good, warm, kind and tender. Where dreams of honest laughter are born, and die because they can't find an escape, cannot be shared. Where the backbreaking loneliness is housed, trying to claw its way out...hoping someone will find a way in...

...This faceless, numbered man in blue can bear the exquisite hurt of wanting...for a special someone...because I have seen the strength of wanting; because I have seen the strength of the double damned and thrice cursed souls who have no one beyond the walls....

Chapter 4
Visiting Days

...I was in prison and you visited me.

Matthew 25:36 (NLT)

Time rolled on very slowly while Bear and I were apart, so I did everything I could to help the time of separation go by more quickly. We only got to visit once every two weeks, a few hours at a time, so we did our best to stay in touch.

The only way to communicate by phone was for Bear to call me collect so our phone bills were shockingly high. We were very much in love and it seemed hard to keep the calls under control. I missed him so much and the months seemed like years at times. We wrote letters and sent cards several times each week.

I longed to have Bear close to me so I came up with an idea that really helped. I found a little tiny stuffed animal bear that would be my point of contact for the rest of Bear's time in prison. I would hold that little Teddy in the palm of my hand and talk to him at night in bed. I would squeeze him tight and pray to God that my big Bear could feel my hugs and hear my voice. I would quote scriptures over my little bear all night long and declare the Word of God over my big Bear to keep him safe.

Many mornings I would find Teddy on the floor or hidden under my covers. I would carry my little Teddy in my purse, praying over him all day long and ask the Lord to be with my big Bear, giving him a special day. Before long, Teddy's head became twisted to the side from all the squeezing I did at night. His face was flat and he wore a funny expression. That didn't matter to me. I just felt so much better with my point of contact enabling me to pray for and *talk* to my Bear. Many times I could sense Bear's emotions and needs as I prayed over that little Teddy. I still have that little Teddy today.

I seemed to live from one visit to the next. Then on visiting day, I was always on a high with excitement to get to see Bear again. I did my best to look good and be a joy for my man to visit. Things like perfume, clean hair and make-up always blessed him after living in prison for so long.

On the way to the prison, it seemed like many times anything that could go wrong, did. Sometimes there was a wreck in front of me that took much longer to make my way to the prison and that cut into my visiting time. Once when visiting Bear, the clothes I had on one time passed just fine, but then another officer wouldn't let me in wearing them a month later. Sometimes the pat searches, drug dogs and metal detectors took forever to get through. There were days when Bear was fighting an attitude within himself for various reasons. It was a hard life to live, having a loved one in prison. I couldn't even tell my boss at my job where I was going each time I went to the prison. One girl had lost her job when she admitted she was married to an inmate.

At first when Bear got back to Walla Walla, the inmates' wives and girlfriends were very unfriendly. I noticed when I got on the shuttle that took me from the parking lot to medium security, that the other ladies ignored me. As much as I would try to make friends, I seemed to be invisible. Finally Bear found out that the inmates had warned their ladies to stay away from me since I was "Mad Dog's lady." They were still living by the old Mad Dog code of fear and it didn't take them long before they realized the old crazy Mad Dog was gone and a new "Bear" had risen in his place. Soon all the ladies were talking to me and I had many friends.

One time Bear got moved to a reception prison for a short time and I had to travel hundreds of miles to go see him. Another time, I sat out in the visiting room for at least a half hour as I waited for Bear to show up.

Teasingly, one of the inmates that was out for his visit saw me by myself and said, "Oh, didn't anyone tell you? Bear was stabbed today and died." I sat there in my chair at the table I was assigned to and felt like I was about to pass out with fear. My heart came up to my throat. It certainly wasn't a joke as that had happened to several other inmates in that unit. The inmate could see my response and was quick to apologize and say that surely Bear would be coming out soon. Would he?

I wondered and for a few minutes fear tried to literally paralyze me. It felt like eternity had passed, by the time Bear got to the visiting room. He was angry when he arrived because a guard had gotten the wrong information and told Bear his visit wasn't in yet. I was on the first shuttle and had been there at least 45 minutes waiting. Almost half of our visiting time was gone, but we were just glad to be together. Despite all the trials and hardships we went through, we had to remain as positive as we could to make sure the joy of the Lord was strong in us.

Visiting days were like a roller coaster of emotions. All of us coming in to visit would be bubbling with excitement that we were about to see our loved one. I would get a surge of joy seeing Bear step into the visiting room. As he arrived, we got one long kiss and hug at the beginning of the visit and one at the end. We would get a couple hours together sitting at a table talking and holding hands, getting something out of the vending machine, and even walking in the tiny yard for a few minutes. Then came the hard part — to hear the officer bark the words, "Visiting is over!"

It was those words that all of us in the visiting room hated to hear. Then came the good-byes as the five minute warning lingered over all of us. Then it was over...we had to leave...my man had to go back to his cell and the whole process of separation and sadness started all over again. All of us visitors would silently make our way back out of the building like a numb herd of cattle, back to the parking lot while the men would quietly head back to their cells in the same way. I can remember those days like they were just last week. There's a lot of pain and loneliness mixed in with all of the love and joy you feel when you go on visiting day. Many days I got back on that shuttle bus to go back to the parking lot with tears streaming down my face. Quiet sobs could be heard throughout the bus from some of the ladies. Many times I would put my hand on a crying lady and share her burden with her as her heart was breaking. I was the blessed one as my man was to be released soon. Some of the ladies were visiting men that would possibly never see the street again.

Chapter 5
Restoration

...and you will be called the repairer of the breach....
Isaiah 58:12 (NASB)

A couple months before Bear got out, I talked his mom Ruth into going with me to visit him in prison. It was hard on her since the last time she saw him was 14 years before in leg irons and chains with dogs on him, and the officers even holding guns on her son. Those days were like a nightmare to Ruth.

She remembered the devastating details too well. "Richard, I'll never be back as long as you're in prison!" she yelled at him as the guards took him away, tears streaming down her face. Bear was known as Mad Dog in those days and it was a name he was proud of. He thought it was keen that *Mad Dog* spelled backwards was *God Dam*. He was damning God and anyone else that got in his way.

"I don't care what you do! I don't even have a mother! My mother died!" Richard screamed at his mother as he was pulled away when he tried to fight his own flesh and blood.

"He's an animal!" she thought to herself, as she saw the guards even strike a blow toward her son, trying to keep him under control. One time Mad Dog even tried to escape for the sole purpose of killing his own mother.

15

He was arrested before he made it to her home. Hate for his mother filled his heart to the point that when he had to fill out any paperwork, he stated that his mother was deceased.

Now 14 years later, Bear was still in prison, but he was a new Christian. He wanted his mother to come visit him. He had written to her and apologized with all of his heart. The family told her not to believe him. "Once a con, always a con," they all agreed.

I had been visiting Bear in prison for nearly seven months now and he had only about three months left to do. I knew he was a new man, but convincing the family that he was different was a huge task. I kept encouraging Ruth to go with me to see him.

"Well, alright. I'll go. But this will be the last time if he shows any anger at all." Ruth still had a lot of fear after her son threatened her life for turning him in years ago.

The day finally came that we started out on the two hour drive to Walla Walla State Penitentiary. It had been nearly 14 years and the last time Ruth saw her son, he was at this same prison. As we drove up to the big gate, Ruth had a worried look on her face and said, "Maybe I should just wait out here for you. I really don't know if he'll be glad to see me or not." I promised her that her son would be ecstatic to see her again.

As we made our way through the pat search and metal detector, I noticed she seemed to be shaking. Her voice cracked as she whispered to me, "How did I let you talk me into this?"

I prayed she would continue on to the visiting room without backing out and making her way back out to the car.

Soon we were waiting in the visiting room for Bear to appear. As he walked in, he gently embraced his mother with tears in his eyes. "I'm so sorry, Mom. I put you through so much. I'm a changed man now. You had to come so you could see for yourself how much I've changed. Jesus has made me a brand new man. I love you, Mom."

As we visited that day, there was lots of laughter and talk of days gone by. The tension was gone. Love and peace ruled the conversation. Many apologies were made. Restoration had come to the relationship. We got up to leave when the visit was declared over and Bear's mom gave him one more giant hug good-bye.

"When you get out, Richard, I'll make you your favorite biscuits and gravy. You'll be home for Thanksgiving! We'll invite all the cousins…" she continued to share her plans with excitement as we walked out the door. As Ruth and I made our way to the parking lot, she turned and looked at me with great joy on her face.

Bear holding one of his mother's biscuits standing next to his mother and Dove.

"It's the first time since he was a little boy that I didn't see death in his eyes. He really has changed!" She gleamed as we pulled out of the prison parking lot.

A few months later, Bear was released. We headed to his mom's house and she greeted him with arms wide open. Biscuits and gravy were on the stove. A big turkey and all of the trimmings were enjoyed at Thanksgiving, with many of the cousins present. Healing of their relationship truly had come.

Chapter 6
Short Timin' Blues

...Though I have fallen, I will rise....

Micah 7:8 (NIV)

Before Bear got out, he was *short timin'* bad. Short timing is the term used when a prisoner is about to get out, but nervous about the changes he'll be faced with. He was so afraid that he wouldn't be able to measure up as a Christian man in the free world. We would talk for hours about what the challenges were going to be when he got out. We would also talk for hours about how wonderful it was going to be. Bear had never had a Christian lady in the free world before, and he was just not sure how to treat one. He would watch "Little House On the Prairie" to try to learn what a Christian type family was supposed to be like. It was the only thing Bear could think of that compared to the family of his dreams.

My thoughts were similar. Only I had never been with a man in the free world that had done so much time. What would he really be like, I wondered? Surely nothing could come up that we couldn't handle, or that our love couldn't endure. I thought the answer to all of our problems was just to get him home. It was so hard having him in prison.

The worst time of the day was always at night. I missed him so much and now in just a few more days I would be in his arms for good. Life would be normal, right? I thought my biggest challenges were with him being locked up, but I was in for a huge awakening because my knight in shining armor was about to come home.

Bear had never been out for more than six months at a time since he went down at the age of eighteen. Now he was forty years old; twenty-two years of his life, mostly behind bars. And that was just adult time. He had a long record of juvenile time as well. When we were in the visiting room two weeks before Bear got out, he got so nervous about his release day, that he broke into a sweat just thinking about it.

"I have to admit, I'm scared," Bear said as we sat at a table in the visiting room.

"Scared of what?" was my gentle reply, fully knowing what he was talking about. Bear and I both knew that if he didn't make it in the free world and just had one incident, he would be locked up for the rest of his life with no hope of getting out. I just knew I had to build him up with encouragement in order for him to make it when he got out.

"You're right. With Jesus and you, I can do anything!" Bear sat up straight in his chair with a fresh new boldness in his voice.

One day Bear called me from the prison with a chuckle in his voice.

"Me and my cell partner have been listening to a tape of this crazy Christian comedian all day. The guy's name is Mike Warnke and he's something else! This Warnke dude is sure helping us all have the joy of the Lord in here."

Never did Bear and I ever imagine someday he and Mike would not only be preaching buddies, but closest of friends.

Right before Bear's release, someone tried to set him up. There's a lot of jealousy toward the guy that's going home, especially someone like Bear that had a lot of old enemies. At one time, Bear had several contracts on his life and some would have killed him for no more than a pack of cigarettes. This time he had favor and it was proven that he was innocent, thank God.

Now, it's only three days and a wake up! Bear called me and gave me the exact count again. Seventy-eight hours, thirty-six minutes and twenty-seven seconds. He sounded excited, but nervous at the same time. He expressed to me that his biggest fear was doing something wrong that would put him back in the joint. We were both flooded with many different emotions.

I faced serious questions from friends and family. Are you sure this is what you want? Do you know you're hooking up with a killer? What if he turns back to his old ways after he's been out for a little while? Some thought I was totally crazy. Many times I had mental questions, but I knew in the depths of my heart that God had put us together and I was determined to walk out what was truly in my heart. Bear had officially proposed to me in prison during one of our visits. We discussed in great length how we wanted to honor the Lord and stay pure after he got out, and that we would get married as soon as we could after his release.

Two days before Bear's release date, a friend took me out for steak dinner. We had a great time, eating and reminiscing about my man coming home. As I was eating, I looked around the restaurant and saw some familiar faces. Isn't that the girl that visits her husband in prison the same days I visit Bear? Here she was snuggled up to another man. She saw me and had a startled, guilty look on her face. Then fear gripped my heart about Bear.

What if he had another woman waiting for him out here? I'd heard many stories of similar situations and about all the games that are played. Bear had admitted to many women being on his visiting list from the past. No, Bear was different now. He had made Jesus Lord of his life. I just had to trust what God had branded in my heart, that I was to stay beside my man no matter what.

As I lay in bed the last night by myself, I was so excited I couldn't sleep. I had to be ready to pick Bear up at 3:30 a.m., the earliest release time on his release date of October 14, 1991. We only had four hours left before he was free. I was staying with a friend, but that was limited. We weren't sure where we would stay after his release. People were afraid of Bear and didn't want him around. Even the local shelter didn't want us because of his felon record. Our dreams were huge and we knew everything would be fine when he got out. We had no idea we would spend the first few months living out of our car, a 1980 Chevette. Surely our love for one another would carry us through anything.

The clock was ticking. It was time to go down to the bus station to pick him up.

I got there early and sat in the parking lot under the streetlight. I waited anxiously for about twenty minutes before I saw the prison shuttle. There he was. This is really it! The thought dashed through my mind as I watched them pull up, "What if something happened this morning and he really didn't get out?" I hadn't heard from him all day. That thought was quickly erased as I spotted my man climbing off the little bus. We walked briskly toward one another, both smiling ear to ear. As we kissed and embraced, both of us quickly looked around making certain there were finally no guards to tell us we couldn't do that. It was really true — my man was finally home!

Chapter 7
First Days of Freedom

We are troubled on every side, yet not distressed; we are perplexed, but not in despair;

Persecuted, but not forsaken; cast down, but not destroyed;

2 Corinthians 4:8,9

As soon as Bear got out, we went looking for a place to stay. No one would let us in as they had heard about this man everyone knew as Mad Dog. The first night Bear was out, we were invited to come spend it with a lady that also had a man inside the local prison with Bear. During one of our visits while Bear was still in prison, I had told her we weren't sure where we'd stay so she graciously told me we could come use her *guest room*. We were delighted to not have to sleep in the car.

It was a tight fit and we would both try to lay down in the back of the hatchback. Bear would then pull the hatch down and nearly every time he would smash his fingers. Then he would repent and ask the Lord to forgive him as he tried to work on his joint vocabulary. We had promised the Lord that we would stay pure and not be physically intimate until we were married. We knew we had to keep our promise so the Lord could bless our union.

That night, as we finally found her address, she let us in and we were ushered into a back room in this extremely tiny house. The little 8' x 10' area was completely empty except for an old mattress on the floor. It was dark, but we could tell by the smell that other creatures had lived there, too. Upon closer examination, we saw animal droppings all over the floor. It appeared that several dogs and cats had stayed in that room before we did. Asking for a broom, we got the room fairly well cleaned up.

As we lay down on the bare mattress with our hearts full of hope and love, we were attacked with crawling biting critters all over us. They were fleas! As we fought on and on with them all night, we were still so thankful that Bear was out of prison. Nothing was going to get us down. We had big dreams and we knew God was bigger than any problem that could show up.

A couple of weeks before Bear was released, he was watching Kenneth Copeland on the prison TV and saw an announcement about the big *Wings of Freedom* motorcycle rally to be held on the KCM grounds in Fort Worth.

"We have to go to Texas," he exclaimed breathlessly calling me collect from prison. "We've got to get full of the Word of God right after I get out of here!"

"Let's go!" I answered, knowing he was right about needing to get full of the Word as soon as he was released.

"I know it will give us the start we need in the free world," Bear continued confidently.

I had saved up a few hundred dollars and we knew it was just enough to get us to Texas to go to the Kenneth Copeland *Wings of Freedom* motorcycle rally. It was a long trip from Washington State, but the little Chevette got good mileage. We knew God wanted us to get there and that He would make a way.

The second day after Bear's release, his parole officer told him he had to pay complete restitution that
week or they'd lock him back up. Bear had such a bad
reputation from the past, threatening to kill everyone in
the system, that they really didn't want him on the outside. It took exactly what I had saved up to pay off the
restitution, so now we had no money for the trip. I held
Bear's head in my lap as he cried and cried, "Will it ever
end? How will we get to the motorcycle rally now?"

As we sat on that couch in tears, suddenly faith rose
up in both of us. Bear sat up and wiped his eyes.
"We've got to get to that rally. I know it's a long shot,
but I'm going to see if I can borrow some money from
my mom. Let's pray right now and ask the Lord to bless
my words." There had been restoration taking place in
their lives, but Bear didn't want to push it and give the
devil any place.

After we prayed, Bear was on the phone talking to
his mom. He explained the whole thing to her and
asked if we could borrow $200. In the past, if Bear
asked for anything, it was a con game and she knew he
would never pay her back. This time, she knew he
would. Slowly, she answered, "I feel strongly about this.
Come on over. I'll get the cash out of the bank today."

Before we knew it, we had money in our pockets
and we were heading to Fort Worth, Texas to the *Wings
of Freedom* motorcycle rally.

Chapter 8
Getting to the Rally

But my God shall supply all your need according to His riches in glory by Christ Jesus.

Philippians 4:19

While traveling to the rally, Bear wanted to stop a lot, try the food and see the sights. We had three days to get there before it started, so he was enjoying the trip. We pulled into several eating places since he was excited about not having to eat joint food anymore. After several polish sausages, corn dogs and ice cream cones, Bear had to find a restroom every few miles. I could literally hear his belly gurgle as we drove on the freeway heading south.

We stopped at one rest area, and I waited in the car. As I sat there, I saw a trucker come running out of the men's restroom, pulling up his pants and doing up his belt. He looked like he was in a huge hurry. He got back up in the cab of his truck and headed out.

A few minutes later, Bear came out to the car.

"I'm not sure if I handled that one right," Bear said kind of sheepishly.

"What do you mean?" I asked.

"Well, there was only one stall in there and there was a guy in it, but I had to go really bad. I jerked the door off the latch and looked at him and said, 'It's either you or me Buddy and I gotta use this thing!' So he took off. I think I scared him pretty bad."

"Oh, well," I mused, wondering how the door looked and realizing that was why the trucker left in such a hurry. I knew I'd have to lean on the wisdom of the Lord to help my man that was so institutionalized. But it was an honor to do so.

As we traveled through Utah on our way to Texas, we stopped to get gas at a truck stop. As Bear was waiting in line to pay for our fill up, I was enjoying looking at some of the souvenirs. I looked up at Bear and saw him put his arm around a man with a bald head. I was wearing a long sleeved red shirt at the time and so was this guy in line. Bear thought it was me. He had his arm around the man and then started snuggling him up close to himself. The man had a petrified look on his face, but didn't move. I walked over to them and Bear saw me. He immediately took his arm off of the man in line.

Dove and Bear on their first road trip together.

"Oh, man!" Bear exclaimed. "I am so sorry! I thought you were my wife!"

"That's O.K.," the guy in the red shirt answered. "I was just hoping you weren't gonna try to kiss me!"

We all had a good laugh at that one!

Finally we crossed over the Texas state line. As we headed south on 35W, we had no idea where we were going. All we knew is that it was somewhere near Fort Worth. Just as we were wondering WHERE in Fort Worth, there it was! A little sign on the side of the road with an arrow said the rally was that direction. We had made it!

As we pulled up to the gate at the rally, there was a sign that said how much it cost to get in. We didn't have enough. My heart sank. I told the gate worker how far we had driven to get there and without hesitation, he said, "Come on in! We'll fix you up."

As we parked our car to the side of the traffic, the gate keeper handed us $20 and told us to get ourselves something to eat. Then he handed us rally t-shirts and caps. God had truly supplied all our needs.

Chapter 9
The Motorcycle Rally

Therefore if any man be in Christ he is a new creature: old things are passed away; behold all things are become new.

2 Corinthians 5:17

We were so amazed at the provision of the Lord that we could hardly contain ourselves. We arrived at the rally not knowing anyone, with hardly any money, but our hearts full of hope and excitement that we made it. People kept coming up to us, and giving us money. Someone bought our meal that night. People were handing us gifts of all kinds. New friends were everywhere as they heard our story of Bear just getting out of prison five days earlier.

That night, awards were given from a big platform. Different trophies were distributed for the winners of the bike show and then one trophy was left. It was called the "Best Blessed" trophy. I'll never forget how we heard Bear's name called that he won that trophy. We had miraculously made it all the way to Texas and now in front of the

Dove holding the "Best Blessed" trophy.

31

whole crowd, we were awarded a big trophy that said we were the *Best Blessed!*

The biker on the platform invited Bear to come up and share from the stage with a microphone. He shared a few moments and told how he had served 22 years in prison and how God got him out. The entire congregation cheered with all their might as they listened to Bear's story. We were truly the best blessed that night! At the close of the meeting, a man prophesied over us about the things the Lord was going to do with us. He said we were going to have a worldwide ministry and that the prisoners around the world would be touched by our testimony and the love in our hearts. We hung on to that dream for dear life even as far away as it seemed that night.

A few months later, the Lord told us to call our ministry *Loving Hearts.* We were called to reach out to the world with the love of God and we were determined to do just that.

During the rally, Bear wanted to meet Kenneth Copeland in person. He had watched Kenneth on the prison TV for years and he always dreamed of getting

Bear at the Kenneth Copeland "Wings of Freedom" motorcyle rally.

close enough to touch this anointed man that all the inmates looked up to. As we were by the big stage where the services were held, Bear saw Kenneth.

"I've got to go meet him. I want to give him this necklace," Bear said as he touched the necklace around his own neck. It was a silver eagle on an arrowhead with silver beads all in a row. Bear had made it while he was in prison. It was a very special piece to him and he wanted to give it to Kenneth as a covenant gift.

As Bear walked toward the back of the stage, there were men guarding the area, but they let Bear go by. They must have sensed that this was a sacred moment for the big biker that was so bold to make his way to Brother Copeland.

Bear stood face to face with Kenneth and bravely introduced himself and then me, as I stood right beside him. Brother Copeland stared at Bear with those Cherokee eyes as only he can. Then Bear shared with him how he had just gotten out of prison five days before and all about the long trip to get there from Washington State. It was as if time stood still as Bear took the necklace off of himself and placed the covenant gift around Brother Copeland's neck.

"I want you to know how much you have meant to me all these years while I was locked up and I represent all the brothers that are still inside. This necklace is my covenant gift to you."

Brother Copeland knew all about covenant and received it with the deep precious earnestness that it was given in. It was a holy moment as the ushers looked on while Bear and Kenneth made the sacred exchange as brothers.

"If you ever need me, I'll be here for you. I mean that," Kenneth shared from his heart as the two embraced one last time. For the next twelve years Kenneth kept his promise and Bear and I conquered more giants, cast out more demons and counted more salvations than we would have ever imagined.

The next day at the rally, Kenneth Copeland had some of his workers interview us with TV cameras. Bear's story had gone around the grounds and the Copelands wanted to capture it for a future time on their TV show, *Believer's Voice of Victory*. It ended up being aired in the spring of the following year.

One of the speakers at the rally that weekend was an ex-outlaw motorcycle guy named Barry Mayson. When Bear looked at him, there was a shocked look on his face. Years before when Bear was connected to an outlaw motorcycle club, there was a contract from *Bear's club* to kill Barry Mayson. He was known as *Barry Barry* at that time. Barry has a great testimony of how he got saved and was sharing that from the stage at the rally. After Barry spoke and the service was over, Bear walked up to him and introduced himself. Bear shared how he tried to escape from prison to kill Barry Barry since they were club rivals. Barry gave Bear a big hug and said, "I heard about you!"

Now Bear and Barry were brothers in the Lord. Bear wanted he and I to be baptized in water together and Barry was just the one to do it.

We all gathered at Eagle Mountain Lake that Sunday afternoon as several were lined up to be baptized that day. Barry Mayson baptized Bear and I together. Bear and I were holding hands as Barry held onto Bear. Both of us went under the water and both came up exactly the same time as if an unseen person was holding us up on the other side. Barry still talks about that baptism and how he had an unseen Helper get us down and back up in the water in a supernatural way.

Chapter 10
The Restaurant

The Lord will perfect that which concerns me....
Psalm 138:8 (NKJV)

After the rally was over, we were invited to stay with a friend we had just met over the weekend. Lots of people had met us at the rally and several wanted to meet us for dinner before we headed back to Washington State.

Eating in a restaurant was new to Bear. A buffet line made Bear nervous because it reminded him so much of the prison chow hall. He was conditioning himself to not hit anyone if he got crowded out in the buffet line. He said he'd rather go to a regular restaurant and order a meal from a menu until he'd been out longer. Fighting with his fists was not only still a temptation, but a way of life in his mind.

Some of the people we met at the rally wanted to get together with us the next week. A pastor and his wife wanted to take us out to dinner in Arlington, Texas at the Red Lobster.

Bear had not been to a fancy restaurant before. He had only been out for a week now. He was used to only eating with a spoon. In prison, knives and forks were contraband and used for stabbing people. Bear was excited about going out to eat and we both dressed up in our best jeans to meet the pastors.

After we all arrived at the restaurant, the hostess seated us. I was aware that Bear needed his back kept to the wall to feel secure so I made sure he was seated as such. We were all visiting and looking at our menus, when I saw a horrified look on Bear's face. Sweat was showing up on his forehead as he squirmed in his chair.

Leaning over to his ear, I whispered, "Are you alright?"

"No!" Bear answered under his breath so no one else could hear.

"What is it?" I pried.

Nervously, Bear quizzed me and said, "Why do we have three forks? I don't have a clue what they're for!"

Now I understood his dilemma. He was fearful of looking foolish in a world he knew nothing about.

"Well, it's simple," I answered, trying to sound confident. Not knowing at that time what the third fork was for either, I had to think fast.

"One is for the salad, one is for the main meal and …the third one is in case you drop one — it's an extra."

"Well, isn't this a nice restaurant," Bear relaxed. As the server came back, he sat up and confidently ordered.

"Ala Carte, please," Bear said, not knowing Ala Carte was not a fancy French dish like he thought. I helped him order a meal and acted like everything was fine. And everything was.

Another time a month or so later, we were with some friends at a different restaurant. This time we all ordered and everyone had gotten their meals except me. Bear looked at me and wondered where my meal was.

I told him I was sure it would be coming along anytime now. He immediately turned angry and stood his big stature up in his seat at the table.

"My wife ain't got her food yet! You better bring it NOW!" He yelled as he slammed his hand down on the table. His fist slammed down so hard that the silverware bounced up and rattled as it fell back.

The entire restaurant filled with people was quiet and staring at us. I'm not sure where they got my plate, but it came fast. We laughed about it later and figured someone else gave up their meal just to keep the *big guy* at peace!

After a few more days in Texas, we headed up to Missouri before we finally made it back to Washington State. My mom was living in Missouri and I wanted her to meet Bear. We finally made it to Mom's and she loved Bear, embracing him and happy that we were together.

How 'bout a Wedding — Or Two?

Then we made our way to the Kansas City area to visit some bikers that we had just met at the rally the

week before. Our biker friends had offered to marry us and host a *biker wedding* for us if we came up. We were blessed with a very special ceremony outdoors — Harleys, bonfire and all. A few months later, we also had a church wedding in Walla

Bear and Dove just married at their "biker wedding."

Walla as all of the family there wanted to enjoy a wedding with us. It was a very special time as Bear's step dad, Willie gave me away. My real dad had passed away several years before and Willie was my first choice. In the old days Bear hated Willie and even sought to kill him at one time. Our *church wedding* really was an example of God's restoration as many were there that had hated the old Richard "Mad Dog" Morgan of the past. It was truly a new day.

Bear's step dad walking Dove down the isle. This is the first time Bear ever had a relationship with his step dad — a testimony to his new life.

Dove and Bear's church wedding.

Chapter 11
Pregnant With a Baby Girl

And this is the confidence we have in Him, that if we ask anything according to His will, He hears us.

And if we know that He hears us, whatever we ask, we know that we have the petitions that we have asked of Him.

1 John 5:14,15 (NKJV)

While Bear was in prison, he talked about someday having a baby girl. He had been hurt in a prison riot in the groin and doctors said he would never father a child again. But Bear said God told him if he believed for a baby, he could have one. "All things are possible to him that believes," Bear would always quote.

"I want a baby girl!" So Bear set his faith for a little girl.

After we'd gotten married and he'd been out for a few months, Bear was getting impatient. One night he said he was putting his faith out there.

"Let's pray over our body parts and speak to them to work!" We prayed and two months later, I found out I was pregnant. We just knew it was our little girl.

We were so excited to know I was carrying his baby. After I was about two or three months pregnant, I started passing a lot of blood and a big clot that looked like a fetus. We were devastated. I went to the doctor the very next day and he confirmed the bad report. He said it was pretty apparent that the baby was gone. The little lump in my stomach was no longer there.

Bear was so angry at the devil. He yelled and pointed to the air and said, "Devil, you'll not steal my baby girl! I demand her to come back, in Jesus' Name!"

Both of us trusted that the Lord had done it once, and He could just help me get pregnant again.

A couple months later, we were traveling across the United States preaching in churches. We happened to be in North Carolina when a 16 year old boy rear ended

Dove and the 1985 Crown Victoria

our car, a 1985 Crown Victoria. We were so proud of our move up from the '80 Chevette and thought we had gone to the Hilton since it was so much bigger and easier to live in. We actually had seats that reclined and we could even stretch our legs out when we slept.

The teenager hit our car with his pick-up and Bear's neck was snapped pretty hard. I felt alright, but the ambulance came and they insisted that we go get checked out. As we were at the hospital, I was able to share Jesus with the family of the boy that hit us. We prayed together and their lives were touched with the love of God. The car ended up being totaled. The family felt horrible about the whole thing, but we knew God had a plan.

As I was being examined at the hospital, Bear and I told the doctor of the miscarriage I had over two months prior. We also shared with him that we were hoping I was pregnant again. I wasn't showing, but we still believed God for a baby.

The doctor put his stethoscope up to my tummy.

"Oh, my!" he exclaimed as he listened. "You're farther along than you think you are!"

At the doctor's request, I went to another room and they did an ultrasound. The results were to be available in a few days. When the day came, I called for the results. The nurse was very sweet and said the results had come back positive! Praise God, I was pregnant again.

"How far along am I?" I asked the nurse on the phone.

"Mrs. Morgan, you're over four months pregnant!" I was stunned. How could I be? The other doctor said I miscarried two months ago. Where did my protruding stomach go?

The very next day, we had to go out and get some maternity clothes. I was shocked. One day I was fitting my clothes and all of a sudden I couldn't wear anything.

We called a few folks we knew to pray for us about our car being totaled, and about our new found pregnancy. We got a call from a ministry the very next day that said they wanted to buy us a little motor home. They gave us an amount to spend, and we found just the perfect motor home that a pastor had for sale. Before we knew it, we were back on the road again, with a much better vehicle to travel in and a baby on the way.

While I was pregnant, we attended a biker fellowship in Missouri. It was a precious home Bible study we

41

were invited to the night before we ministered at a church in that town. During the worship, the guy who led singing and playing guitar, stopped singing and looked right at me.

"God just told me you're carrying a baby girl." Now this guy had never talked to us before and didn't have a clue what we'd been through.

"And she's got golden hair and will love to worship the Lord," he added. Then he went right back to leading everyone in song with his guitar. I'll never forget the peace that filled the place that special moment.

The very next day, Bear preached at the local church. As soon as the service was over, a man with a very demonic look on his face came over to me as I sat on the front row.

"God told me to tell you that the baby you're carrying is a boy!" he spouted with a frown. "And he wants you to know if you don't take care of yourself, you'll kill the child before it's even born!"

I knew that wasn't right! Of all people, I was always taking care of myself. Bear called me *Mrs. Healthy* because I always ate what was right. It just showed me to follow the peace of God when people tried to give a *word*. Many times a *word* is no more than the enemy trying to put fear in your heart.

A month later, we had an ultra sound done and found out our baby was indeed a little girl. Bear sang *Jesus loves Me* to her nearly every night before he went to sleep by putting his face near my stomach. We decided on the name Micah, partially because one of the workers at Kenneth Copeland Ministries was a lady named Mika Simpson. She was always there for us whenever we needed to call her and several times prayed over us in the early days of Bear's walk in the free world.

Chapter 12
Our Baby Girl is Born

Behold, children are a heritage from the Lord, The fruit of the womb is a reward.

Psalm 127:3 (NKJV)

At last, I was only a couple weeks from my due date. Bear woke up one morning and said he wanted Micah to be born that day. I told him that was crazy — we still had a couple weeks to wait and that God had already ordained the perfect time for her to be born. He said he was tired of waiting for her and he was using his faith since he wanted to see his baby girl *today*. Wouldn't you know it — I went into labor that day — about *two hours later!* Micah Faith was born with one hand up, coming out with her head, like she was praising the Lord. Micah means "who is like our God," — it's a praise unto the Lord, and Faith because that's what it took to believe for her. She was born at the birthing center in Grand Prairie, Texas, November 13, 1992. Bear held her up to

Newborn Micah Faith Morgan with her parents.

Bear holding his newborn baby Micah.

the Lord as soon as she came into this world, and dedicated her back to God; promising to raise her in the nurture and admonition of the Lord all the days of our lives. It was a very special time in that birthing room while Kellie Copeland's *Lullaby* tape was playing in the background. I was so blessed to have my baby in my arms.

When Micah was around four weeks old, we were on a radio broadcast in Georgia. A lady that happened to speak right before we were to go on the station live said she would be glad to watch Micah as she slept in her little infant seat. After we did our radio broadcast, we got back out to the lobby where the woman was keeping our baby for us.

"Do you know who this is?" the woman was crying as she asked. "This is a very special child..." She went on and on about how exceptional Micah was to the Lord. I'll never forget the seriousness of the expression on her face as she kept saying it over and over.

Micah's dedication service with Jeff Fenholt.

Micah at three months old, with her parents going to a "Biker Sunday" at a church in Texas.

When Micah was only six weeks old, we happened to go see Mike Barber live at the TBN television studio in Dallas. Carlton Pearson was hosting that night. During a break in the interview with Mike, one of the floor workers was sharing with Pastor Pearson about Bear's testimony and how we were in the audience. Pastor Pearson then asked to see the baby of the guy that had served so much time in prison. The next thing we knew, Micah was on national TV.

Daddy Bear and seven month old Micah

Carlton shared about her daddy and his story as Micah just looked up and gurgled at him the whole time. Bear had been full of racism in prison, but he thought he'd gotten over his old feeling of being prejudiced. When Carlton Pearson looked at Micah and said, "Come to *Uncle Carlton*," on national TV, Bear realized he still had some old hate to deal with. Who would've guessed his baby girl, held by our black brother Pastor Pearson, would be the one that helped bring it to the surface.

A few years went by and we were at the Christian Retreat in Bradenton, Florida. Micah was only four years old when she sat with us in our hotel room playing with her doll. As Bear was preparing for his next sermon, Micah looked up and shared with him.

Four year old Micah on stage with Mom and Dad at the Brandenton, Florida Christian Retreat.

Daddy Bear and four year old Micah at Christmas time.

"Daddy, remember when I left Mommy's tummy and went to Heaven? Jesus brought me back so I could be with you." We knew that our daughter surely had a special call on her life and God had entrusted us as stewards.

Chapter 13
Attack of the Enemy

...When the enemy shall come in like a flood, the Spirit of the Lord shall lift up a standard against him.

Isaiah 59:19

As Bear and I were traveling, we met people that wanted to help us in the ministry. One guy that we thought we knew fairly well, offered to keep our accounting while we were on the road. He asked for our partner list, and other information concerning the ministry. We were so grateful to get the help, we really didn't pray like we should have about him taking some of the load for us.

Soon it was evident we had made a huge mistake to allow him to help. Our t-shirt supplier called us and wanted to know if it was alright with us if he changed the logo on our ministry shirt. He had gotten a call from the guy that was helping us that we wanted things changed. We had never even talked to him about changing anything. This guy was working so hard for the devil, he even called the ministry that had first ordained us and lied and told them we were in trouble with the IRS. Then he called our partner list and told everyone he could (before we found out about it) that we were no good and to stop giving to our ministry. It was a nightmare. Especially when the ministry we were ordained under at that time called and said they didn't want any heat on them, so consider ourselves not covered by them any longer. We realized later that we didn't want to be ordained by them anyway.

But at that time Bear and I felt crushed. People we loved and trusted were leaving our sides. The money had almost stopped coming in and we counted on our partners to keep us going on the road. We felt weak and defeated. Bear and I literally got on our faces and sought the Lord for several days. The devil was trying his best to kill *Loving Hearts Ministry* while it was still in the baby stage.

We heard that the guy that was trying to damage our ministry had even called Kenneth Copeland Ministries to give us a bad name. He made the mistake of calling them though, since they could see through the devil's attack and were supportive of Bear and I all the way.

We had been planning for weeks to attend the West Coast Believer's convention in Los Angeles, California. It was summer time and we had promised all of the kids — Bear's son, Rick and my three boys, Riley, Ty and Lain, plus Micah was a seven month old baby — that we would take them all to Disneyland while we were in California. Now we had the kids looking forward to a trip that didn't look like could possibly happen.

Bear and I looked at each other and agreed God was still on the throne.

"Let's just go," Bear said. "We have enough money to get there." That's always how we did things. If God said go, we just went.

We didn't tell the kids we didn't have any money to go to Disneyland. We just told them to believe God for it so it would keep their hopes high and let their excitement remain. We drove the little motor home from

Washington State to Los Angeles and had just enough money remaining to spend one night in a motel.

We got everybody dressed and found the convention center where the meetings were being held. We looked forward to be able to soak under the anointing after such a battle had gone on.

The boys went to Superkids and we found our way up the bleachers to sit down in the auditorium. Brother Copeland was just coming out to preach. After the session was started, Bear got up to go to the bathroom. We were seated halfway up the bleachers on the left side of the platform.

As soon as Bear started walking back up to our seat, Brother Copeland looked up at him and said, "Bear Morgan, come here!" Bear quickly made his way down to the stage in front of thousands of people. I sat in the bleachers holding Micah.

Brother Copeland mentioned that the Lord told him that he would be praying over a biker today at the meeting and when he saw Bear, he realized he was the one.

"You've been through lots of battles," Brother Copeland spoke as he stood face to face with Bear. "But this battle you've gone through lately has been a mean one. It's only from the devil, but you've won this battle and you'll win 'em all."

Kenneth finished with a prayer over Bear. Then his last words were, "And the Lord wants you to know that He's pleased with the way you've decided to raise your child."

As Bear walked back up to where I was seated, we were both in tears. God had given us a big hug and the confidence in knowing we were right in the middle of His will. As soon as Bear sat back down next to me, a man that sat in the seat behind us handed Bear a check for $500. We'd never seen him before and still don't know who he was. Kenneth Copeland Ministries offered to cash the check for us. We were so blessed. We knew the kids could go to Disneyland as the Father's provision had come.

As the meeting was over for the afternoon, we were walking around the convention center and others handed us money. We not only had money to go to Disneyland, but we were able to get a motel within walking distance to the meetings for the rest of the week that had a swimming pool for the kids. We even ended up having enough money to also take the kids to Knott's Berry Farm and plenty to get back home on. It was a summer adventure they would never forget.

Left to Right: Riley, Rick, Lain, Ty holding four year old Micah

Chapter 14
Bible School? Not Me!

The steps of a good man are ordered by the Lord: and He delights in his way.
Psalms 37:23 (NKJV)

In the summer of 1994, we heard that Brother Jerry Savelle was starting a Bible school near his ministry headquarters in Crowley, Texas. Never thinking that might be something for us to look into, our pastor, George Pearsons, of Eagle Mountain International Church, wanted to meet with us. It was July when he sat with us and shared his heart.

"I've been praying for you and I really believe you should consider going to Jerry Savelle's Bible School this fall." Pastor George seriously seemed to think it was something we should strongly pray about.

Bear remarked with an eyebrow raised. "Me? Go to Bible school? I didn't even finish the sixth grade. I'd never make it."

"Well, I really believe you should at least pray about it, Bear."

"Alright, I will," Bear said without really meaning it. "But I can tell you right now, our speaking schedule is full for travel and there's no way financially that we could go. But I promise I'll pray about it."

We got back home and Bear kept his promise. He took my hands in his and said, "Well, let's pray about going to Bible School like Pastor George said. But I know we're not going. We're scheduled to travel and we leave for North Carolina next week."

That night we got a call from the church in North Carolina. "Pastor says he's sorry, but he has to cancel the meeting you were scheduled to speak at. There's been a family emergency and we just can't do it."

The next day, another speaking engagement was cancelled. Out of five churches we were supposed to travel to and speak at, four cancelled their meetings within two weeks.

Pastor George saw us at church that following Sunday and asked, "Have you prayed about going to Bible school?"

Bear told him that he prayed and told God that if both of our tuitions were paid, he would go. The next day we got a phone call.

"Your tuitions have both been paid," the voice said from Jerry Savelle's office. "We need you to come and pick up your applications, fill them out and bring them back in."

Bear was upset at first. "I can't go to Bible School! What am I going to wear?" He only wore a leather vest, black jeans and t-shirts. Being a biker, black was really all that he had. He heard there was a dress code at the Bible school and he didn't think he could ever measure up to it. Bear was starting to sweat at the thought of a classroom situation.

We got another call. "Hey Bear," the voice said on the other line. "Pastor George wanted me to let you know I'm taking you shopping for suits, shoes and ties for Bible School. I'll meet you at the Men's Wearhouse tomorrow." It was Leon Cantrell, the praise leader at EMIC.

Now there was no turning back and Bear and I were really going to the new Bible School. Brother Jerry called it his *School of World Evangelism*. The next time we went to church, Pastor George saw us and handed Bear a bag.

"Here, Bear. We wanted to make sure you had some special ties. They were Brother Copeland's dad's ties — A. W. Copeland. He wanted you to have them."

Bear was so blessed. He never imagined having such a special gift. He cried on the way home from church.

"What an honor," Bear shared with emotion. "At least my neck will be anointed. Now I just gotta learn how to tie the silly things!"

Chapter 15
Bible School, Here We Come!

I can do all things through Christ who strengthens me.
Philippians 4:13 (NKJV)

There we were in the charter class at *J.S.M.I. School of World Evangelism.* Bear looked great in his new suits, but he always went home as fast as he could to change into his jeans. He was excited to be there, but very insecure about the classes. He didn't know how to take notes. He got sleepy when the classes were in session. Instead of writing notes during speakers, he would draw little "I love you" notes to me. I prayed a lot that he would pass and stay in school. I loved going, but didn't want to go by myself.

At that time, we were staying with some people near Crowley. They loaned us a 20 foot travel trailer to live in. It was really small and everyday Bear would bump into something and hurt himself. It was just too small for a big guy like him, but we were very thankful for a place to stay.

I had to lock myself up in the tiny little bathroom to study for school. It had a little light and I would sit on top of the toilet and read at night. Bear said he didn't need to study. He told me one day during the first month of school that if God wanted him to know something, He would tell him in his sleep.

Finally, the first tests were due. Bear wanted to cheat and look at my answers. I knew I couldn't let him, but he was very convinced that this was how he was going to make it through and not flunk. In prison, Bear had always bluffed his way through everything.

Bear and Dove in class at J.S.M.I.

He even got his GED in prison by trading it for a carton of cigarettes.

"The rules say wives and husbands can work together!" He spouted under his breath.

"But that's not during the tests," I explained. "I can't let you cheat. The Lord told me not to." And with that, I got up and moved to a different place in the classroom.

Bear was furious with me! He threw his pencil down so hard on the table that it bounced up and almost stabbed a guy in the back that was sitting in the row in front of us. Bear didn't speak to me for the rest of that day.

I prayed all afternoon asking the Lord how to handle it. God gave me the answer.

I asked Bear if he would talk to me late that afternoon and he said he would. A soft answer always turned away Bear's wrath.

"You're smart and you don't seem to think you are," I told him. "Remember when you played poker in prison? You won a lot because you have a sharp mind.

God's going to teach us how you can use your sharp mind in school."

I shared with him how he *can do all things through Christ who strengthens him.* He started memorizing scripture that built him up. We proclaimed that he had the mind of Christ. I taped scriptures around the house that were confidence builders.

That week the Lord helped me think of jingles and little sayings to better memorize some of the required lists. Within just a few days, Bear could quote the entire books of the Bible just by the jingle we made up. He was so happy. His grades climbed up quickly and by the time school was just about over, he even got a higher score than I did on one of the finals.

Jesse Duplantis was one of the guest speakers that year and he prophesied over Bear and I. Word for word, Jesse said,

"Oh, Father, thank you, Lord, for this special couple, special people, special couple. Oh Father, thank you, Jesus that you have made him a Bear. A person of great power, great strength. Lord, both of them today are here by divine appointment. You made her Dove. Oh, what a balance. A Bear and a Dove. One walking the earth and one flying in the sky. Nothing can be missed, because one sees from above and one sees from below. Lord, let this anointing flow. God let them go forth with what they learn from here. Straight to the skies and straight into the land 'cause *one's a Bear* and *one's a Dove.* I thank you, Lord, I thank you that you have called these people."

Chapter 16
Bible School, Here We Are!

For the commandment is a lamp; and the law is light; and reproofs of instruction are the way of life.

Proverbs 6:23

There were many challenges that arose during our time at school. The pews that Bear broke while sitting in chapel, his new shoes that slid on the floor and made him fall, and the days he sweated through the tests, just to name a few.

Bear was also intimidated by some of the teachers. One teacher walked around the classroom one day during class, looking over the student's shoulders to see if everyone was taking proper notes. Bear steamed as she came by our table.

"You think I'm dumb or something?" Bear snorted grabbing his notebook so she couldn't see it.

"Not at all, Bear. I was just trying to help," she answered. Bear squirmed in his chair with no comment as the classroom got extremely quiet.

Then there were several adventures with Dean Todd Powers. I was so thankful that Brother Todd walked in wisdom around Bear. He knew that he and Bear had come from two different worlds that were complete opposites. Brother Todd had come from Rhema, a Bible school in Tulsa, and Bear had come from the school of crime and prison.

One day it was announced that whoever could, was to go to an outreach in Houston. The students were to sleep in a dorm and minister during a conference, and do an outreach on the streets.

Bear wanted to go. I stayed home to watch several children of students and to be with our own family.

After the students had been gone for a day or so, I got a phone call from Bear in Houston.

"Well, I'm coming home. I just quit school!" Bear said on the other end like he was proud of himself.

"You what?!" I asked in shock.

"Yeah, you'd been proud of me. Brother Todd made me so mad and I didn't even hit him. All I did was throw my name tag in his face and tell him to stick it where the sun don't shine! I told him I don't need him or his stinkin' school!"

After a few more minutes on the phone, I finally talked Bear into going back and apologizing to everyone. He explained what made him mad and I drew on the anointing to help me convince him he needed to go back. I prayed over him and he finally said he guessed he'd go back and apologize. I just prayed that they would receive him back.

About two long hours later, Bear called me again.

"Well, I'm back in school. I went back and apologized. Brother Jerry (Savelle) was there, and Jesse (Duplantis) and they said I couldn't quit. Then I said I was sorry to Brother Todd."

Whew, I was so thankful for men of God that could see the treasure in a man that the world had thrown away. That was another day that true *agapé* love changed Bear's destiny.

Chapter 17
Ending the Racism

If someone says, "I love God," and hates his brother, he is a liar; for he who does not love his brother whom he has seen, how can he love God whom he has not seen?

1 John 4:20 (NKJV)

One day we were in chapel before we were to go to class. The Spirit of God was really moving and several of the students were weeping before the Lord. Bear looked at me and whispered, "I have to get rid of the last bit of racism in my heart. I'm supposed to wash that black sister's feet in front of everyone." Bear pointed to Faye Eikner, a sister in our class.

As I confirmed Bear's desire to go ahead and do it, he asked one of the class helpers if they could get him a pan of water and a towel. Soon the equipment to do a foot washing was there. Bear asked this sister to come to the front and sit down. As he cried and washed her feet, he confessed his sin of being prejudiced after years of prison where it was a way of life. She cried with him and the entire chapel rejoiced in God's goodness. Chains fell off of many that day.

Then a couple years later, we joined the group from J.S.M.I that was going to Africa. I had already been once, and couldn't wait for Bear to go with me to experience the trip for himself. We believed God for both of us to go and the very last week all of the money came in.

While we were in Kenya, Bear had a great time. He fell in love with the people there. They are a very special nation and very hungry for the things of God. One of the customs the Kenyans do, is to hold hands with those of the same gender as a gesture that they accept you and are your friend.

One day we were walking in Nairobi to share the Gospel with folks on the streets. A man from the Kenyan church that had joined us, walked next to Bear and grabbed his hand as they went to the park. I was stunned as I watched my husband walk hand in hand not only with a man, but a black man as well.

When Bear came back to the meeting spot, he looked at me and grinned.

"I know I'm free of any prejudices now. I walked for an hour hand in hand with a black man and it didn't even bother me!"

Praise God for the freedom that Jesus brought mankind.

Mission Trip to Africa

Chapter 18
Our Own House

Trust in the Lord with all of your heart, And lean not to your own understanding;

In all your ways acknowledge Him, And He shall direct your paths.
Proverbs 3:5,6 (NKJV)

After school had been going for a couple months, in prayer one day I heard the Lord say that he had our own house for us. We had been living in the little travel trailer, but with the size of people we were, it seemed to get smaller each day. We believed God for our own house.

The day I heard in my spirit that *our house was here,* I talked to Julie Powers, who worked in the office of the school. I asked her if she knew of any houses available.

"You know what? I just heard of one yesterday. Let me make a call," Julie said as she got immediately on the phone.

After speaking with someone for a few minutes, she finished the conversation saying that Bear and I were good students and they would recommend us. After Julie got off the phone, she said we were to meet with the land manager of the house the next day.

Wow, the Lord was working fast. We had no money, but we knew if the Lord said He had a house for us, then He would supply it.

The next day came and I just knew someone would hand us money or there would be some in the mail to help us get our house. We were to meet the lady at our house after school that day. The house was for rent and was empty. They were just going to put an ad in the paper that week.

We were excited as we followed the directions and arrived on time. The house was perfect. It was only ten minutes from J.S.M.I. and all of the kids would have their own rooms. It was much more than we could ask for. We were excited. The lady that showed it to us, Deanna Daniel, was precious and Bear told her his testimony about being in prison. We were hoping that wouldn't scare her off, but thought it would be best for her to hear it from us. She set it straight right then that a man's past was just that and she believed everyone needed another chance to do right. She liked us and let us know the house was ours.

"I'll meet you back here tomorrow after school and give you the key to move in. Then you can pay me the amount we agreed on." She had no idea we didn't even have a dollar to put on that house. They did agree to not charge us a deposit since we had committed to finish some painting that needed to be done inside.

The next day came and still no money showed up. We were to meet Deanna at one o'clock after school. I just knew money would show up somehow. All morning during classes I wondered who would be giving us the money we needed. Nobody knew that we didn't have the money, but we shared with everyone that God had blessed us with a house. We hurried to the mail box before we were to meet at the house. Nothing. Not even a five dollar check. Discouraged, we headed to our new house.

We pulled up in the driveway and Deanna wasn't there yet. Bear and I both got out and paced at the back door.

"What will we tell her when she gets here?" Bear said with a worried voice.

"I don't know, but I do know God said He had a house for us and we know this is it. The Lord will just have to give us the right words to say to her." I was trying to reassure Bear, but I didn't have any ideas either of what to say to her.

"It's gonna sound real great to tell her, 'yeah, I'm an ex-con and I want this house, but I have no money.'" So we grabbed hands and prayed together, asking God for wisdom.

Just as we were wondering what we were to tell her, Deanna drove up. Bear and I were standing in the driveway so we stepped aside to give her room to park. She pulled up right next to where we were standing and rolled her window down. She looked pale and was humped up over the steering wheel.

"Here's the key so you can move in," she said as she threw it out of her car window and hit Bear in the chest. He caught the key in mid air.

The House in Crowley, Texas.

"I can't stay. I've got the flu or something. I'll just be back next week to get the money from you." And with that, she rolled her window back up and drove away.

Bear and I looked at each other and squealed. God had done it again!

We started moving in that day without a dime. And when Deanna came the next week for the rent money, it was all there to give her!

Chapter 19
The Harley

Give, and it will be given to you: good measure,
pressed down, shaken together, and running over will
be put into your bosom. For with the same measure
that you use, it will be measured back to you.

Luke 6:38 (NKJV)

As we went through J.S.M.I., God's unending supply
always showed up. I found brand new dresses and
suits in our van. Money would show up in envelopes
on our seat at school. Some partners in the ministry
upped their giving knowing we were going to school.
We found groceries at our doorstep. Stores started calling us with excess bread and goods so we started putting our own *food bank* together on our back porch to
help other students in need. We gave all the time, not
only money, but clothes, food and even let people come
in to our house to stay. Some were fresh out of prison,
some were off the streets. We wanted to help and be a
blessing to others as our God had blessed us. One
night I counted the people that were sleeping in our
home that were not our family and it totaled 17. The
love of God was strong in our hearts and we wanted to
share it with whosoever would come.

During the middle of our first year at J.S.M.I., we
were standing in faith for our rent to be paid. It always
came in, even if a few times it was late. Deanna always

gave us a positive response and assured us that she knew the rent would be there soon. Many times she was like the pillar we needed to lean on as she spoke life into us when times got tough.

It was during one of those times that the rent was late, that Brother Jerry Savelle said he needed to speak with us. Immediately Bear was wondering if it was over the rent we owed. J.S.M.I. had some strict rules that you couldn't owe others very much or it would be a cause to be discharged from school. Integrity was important.

Nervously, we met with Brother Jerry and Sister Carolyn.

"Bear, the Lord told me to give you something I have...my Harley," Brother Jerry politely spoke. Bear and I were stunned and silent.

"What did you say?" Bear asked.

"The Lord told me to give you my Harley," Brother Jerry repeated. "To me it's been a toy, but the Lord told me for you it will be a tool."

After the shock, we were able to regain our composure enough to thank them and then go out and scream for joy. The next day, Brother Jerry had the bike all shined up and ready to pick up. It was his *1995 Heritage Softtail*. It was brand new, with only 90 miles on it. We could hardly think straight during classes as we were told the bike would be presented to us at the close of school that day. Finally, classes were over. Everyone headed out to the parking lot where the Harley was. Brother Jerry presented it to us with very special words. Then as Brother Jerry prayed over the bike, the last thing in his prayer was, "Harley, go win souls!"

I had a long skirt on, but still managed to get on the bike with Bear. As we rode it home and another student drove our car home for us, we talked above the roar of the engine. Thoughts flooded our minds. We knew we had no money at all. Brother Jerry had asked us to change the insurance right away. We weren't sure how we would even put gas in it when the gas ran out. What would the landlords say when they saw a new Harley in the carport? Especially since we still owed rent and the next month's rent would be due soon. Would they think we spent our rent money on the bike? The scripture came to us that, "The blessing of the Lord it makes us rich and He adds no sorrow with it." We weren't going to let the devil steal our joy. Praise God, the money came in to change the insurance in three days. Our rent money showed up in the mail. God was always faithful.

Jerry Savelle dedicating his 1995 Heritage Softtail Harley into the ministry of Bear and Dove.

Brother Jerry prayed over the bike that it would go and win souls, and it did. That very week, Bear and I were on the bike when we went to the local grocery store in Crowley. I went in to shop by myself as he wanted to stay with the Harley. While I was in the store, a man walked up and remarked about the beautiful bike.

"The Lord gave me this," Bear explained. "It's a tool for Him."

The man immediately started sharing his story with Bear. He had been a pastor at one time and fell away from the Lord due to discouragement. Bear asked if he could pray for him. The man said yes and that he wanted to rededicate his life back to Jesus.

Bear prayed for him right in that grocery store parking lot and the angels in Heaven rejoiced. A soul had been touched because of the Harley.

Chapter 20
God Said Go

And He said unto them, "Go into all the world and preach the gospel to every creature."

Mark 16:15 (NKJV)

We graduated from the charter class of J.S.M.I. in May of 1995. Then we went back out on the road preaching in churches, bike rallies, and anywhere the Lord would send us. Sometimes they were big churches, such as The Carpenter's Home church in Florida, which was one of the largest in  the U.S. Sometimes they were small churches like the street church we preached at in Houston, Texas. It was

J.S.M.I. Ordination Service

an abandoned building with a big hole in the roof, windows all knocked out, with prostitutes and drug addicts peering in, and only five people came inside, but we were faithful and preached our hearts

71

out. A man came to the altar and gave his heart to Jesus that night.

One service we ministered in, the people met in a chicken house. It was an old broiler house with potbelly pigs and goats running around the pulpit. We preached everything that was in us like we were at a stadium. People gave their hearts to the Lord. We were faithful no matter what and always saw the Lord at work in lives everywhere.

The first five years that Bear was out of prison, we had preached in hundreds of churches, rallies, youth groups and prisons all over the U.S.

Dove and Bear preaching at Randy and Paula White's Church in Florida.

Ministering at outdoor meetings.   *Sharing God's love one-on-one.*

The Heritage Softtail packed for it's first mission trip.

It was in 1996 that we heard the Lord say he wanted us to go to Daytona Beach, Florida on the bike. We weren't sure how we were going to get there, but we knew we had heard from God. We had a good house sitter to stay with the kids so that end was taken care of. All we knew is that God said to go, so we started packing. The day before we left, we still needed bungee cords for the load to be tied down with. We had $20 and that was it. The bungees cost $9. Now we had only $11 to our name. I packed peanut butter, crackers, hot chocolate and cheese. We had our clothes, a small tent, we had our bedroll and I even packed my beads so I could do my beaded hair wraps when we got to bike week. God had given me a creative way to minister to ladies and also make some money at rallies. I did a hair wrap with beads and called them *Dove Tails*. It was a great way to get women to sit and share their hearts with me, and then I could pray with them and just love on them.

The Heritage Softtail was packed and we were ready to head out. It was loaded, but we knew we could be gone up to three weeks. It was a long trip to Florida from Crowley. We said our goodbyes and hit the road. As I sat behind Bear on the bike, I thought to myself how I wish I had some gum, but I didn't want to tap in to the $11 dollars we had. We knew we heard the Lord say to go, and we trusted that He would get us there.

It was a little cool that morning and Bear turned his head so I could hear him speak above the engine. We were only a couple miles from the house.

"I need to pull over and put my gloves on," he said loudly. Just as we were pulling in to a business parking lot before we hit the freeway, I saw a pack of gum on the ground. It was brand new and my favorite kind. It was one of those big packs, too. I jumped off the bike after Bear parked it to get his gloves.

"Where you going?" He asked.

"God gave me some gum!" I exclaimed, as I ran to pick it up. So we both got back on the bike, already sensing the provision of the Lord for this trip.

Chapter 21
Getting to Bike Week

And without faith it is impossible to please Him....
Hebrews 11:6 (NASB)

Just as we had gotten to the edge of Texas, near Shreveport, we were almost out of money. We stopped at McDonald's to get warmed up. I had packed lots of hot chocolate, knowing we could get free hot water and mix our chocolate ourselves. We got our free water and sat down at a table. We were opening our hot chocolate packets, when a man stepped up to our table.

"I see you're Christian bikers," he smiled. "It really blesses me to see tough guys show off Jesus. I pastor a church right down the road from here." The pastor then joined our table and shared briefly with us about his church and his love for Jesus. After a few minutes, he got up and handed us a 20 dollar bill. "The Lord said to give you this."

And it was like that the rest of the trip. We were excited to follow the leading of the Lord and watch Him provide. We rode the bike as far as we could, then would sleep on park benches when we were too tired to keep going. One night was too cold to sleep outside so we made a little bed with chairs in the café of a gas station. After working on getting chairs together, we laid down only to realize we were just as cold in the building as we were outside. They had the air conditioning on. Being too tired to go on, we got everything we could off the bike and put it on — gloves, scarves, ski masks, leathers, and tried to sleep on our make shift bed. I'm sure we were a sight when people came in to pay for their gas. We did get a little sleep there, but were glad when the sun came out and warmed us up as we rode the bike the next day.

The provision of the Lord kept showing up. One time when we filled up with gas in Mississippi, we went in to pay for it and the lady said someone already had. We stopped by our friend, *Mac Gober's Canaan Land Bible Training Center* when we went through Alabama. We spent the night with Bubba, Mac's director, and his wife, Paulette. It was so nice to get a shower and sleep on a real bed. No one knew we hadn't been getting motels along the way. No one needed to.

Just as we were ready to head back out toward Daytona Beach, Bubba said Mac had called and asked if we needed anything. Bear told him how the bike tire in back was getting thin and the bike needed an oil change. We were directed to go to the local Harley shop to get all fixed up. As we left Canaan Land, Bubba handed us some money. "Here, the Lord said to give you this." We looked and it was $100. We were so thankful to be so well taken care of. God's provision was at every turn.

A few miles down the road, we got to the Harley shop. They were having an anniversary celebration and had a huge supply of food and drinks free to all customers. We felt like the Kings kids that we were, enjoying popcorn, nuts, and snacks of all kinds and eating all we could hold. Bear got a good nap in the waiting area. Soon the bike was finished and we hit the road again, full and well rested.

When we got to our destination, we had $65 in our pockets. We left home with $11, and God met every need.

Chapter 22
Bike Week

And it shall come to pass, that whosoever shall call on the name of the Lord shall be saved. Acts 2:21

Here we were, at *Daytona Beach Bike Week*. Bikes were everywhere and the sound of Harleys filled every minute of the days and nights of the week we were there. We heard there were 500,000 bikes that year. People came from around the world. We had been invited to stay with people we didn't know, that were partners of Kenneth Copeland Ministries. They had heard of Bear's testimony and passed the word on that they'd love to host us. We called them when we got into town and they met us at a restaurant. It was all planned for us where we were to stay, the red carpet had been rolled out again. The generosity of the people was more than we could have asked for. They had a great bed for us, a hot shower, lots of wonderful food and shared anointed fellowship each day we were there.

The next day, we drove the bike among the thousands of people to meet with some people we had met at a rally in Texas. They were vendors and they said they might have a spot for us to set up my "Dove Tail" booth in front of the Iron Horse Saloon. When we found them they were excited to share their spot. We quickly set up my beads and right away women lined up to get their *Dove Tail*. God's favor was strong. At one time, 35 women were in line to get a *Dove Tail*. Ladies came to me drunk, but wanted prayer. Some wanted to give their lives to Jesus for the first time, and some wanted to rededicate their lives.

Bear kept busy praying for people that walked by. One man had a heart attack while we were there and several came to get Bear to pray. Another man got run over and killed just in front of us and Bear was asked to be the *Chaplain* among the bikers for the rest of that week on our side of town.

Among the thousands of partiers that had come to Bike Week, many were getting touched by the love of God. Some couldn't speak English so we guessed which beads they wanted. A few men wanted *tails* in their Manchu or mustache. Andy Matthews had mailed a box of *Faith to Faith* devotionals to our host home so I gave one to every person that got a *Dove Tail*. I charged $1.50 per inch doing *tails* for five days straight and made over $950 dollars. Besides the lives getting touched with the Gospel, we were able to send money home to pay rent and we had money to get home on. The provision of the Lord exceeded anything we could have hoped for.

Chapter 23
Murder Spirit

Whoever hates his brother is a murderer, and you know that no murderer has eternal life abiding in him.
1 John 3:15 (NKJV)

It was during the Kenneth Copeland Believer's Convention that next summer that Bear was going through some challenges with people. He was dealing with anger toward someone who didn't keep their word. Bear always said in prison, *your word was your bond.* If your word was no good, you were no good. People's lives were at stake in prison and he'd seen several inmates killed because of somebody not keeping their word.

We had been at the Believer's Convention for a couple days and were sitting in the meeting listening to Jesse Duplantis. Each year it was held at the Tarrant County Convention Center and thousands of people came from all over the world. We always did our best to attend as much as we could.

Jesse was just about to finish his session when he looked up at our side of the convention center and said, "Someone on this side of the building has hate in your heart that has formed into a murder spirit. You need to come down here and let me pray for you and you'll be delivered tonight. I'll wait for you," Jesse finished. He kept looking up toward where we were sitting.

I looked up at Bear and said, "I'm glad you're not like that anymore."

He looked back at me and with a sad look on his face said, "I think it's me Jesse is talking about. I've been so mad at this person, I've even been wondering how I could kill him."

It shocked me to the core when I heard Bear say those words. I could hardly believe it. Here he was a graduate of J.S.M.I. and wanted to murder someone. I was glad he wanted deliverance though. "You need to follow God," I coaxed. "Lots of lives are in the balance."

Everyone around us looked surprised as they saw Bear make his way down to the front where Jesse was waiting. Being the big man that he was, many people moved out of the way like they feared him now.

Bear was dressed in his usual biker attire and on the back of his vest had the airbrushing of big words of our ministry, Loving Hearts Ministry. The video cameras were on him now and you could see him in the big screen overhead. I thought to myself how ironic to have Loving Hearts Ministry on your back, but murder in your heart. I was irritated at the situation at first, but glad he was yielding to the anointing to get rid of it.

"What a humble man," I finally thought as I watched Bear walk down to Jesse.

Bear got in front of Jesse and stood tall. Jesse looked up at the man a foot taller than he and said, "Bear, I had no idea it was you!"

Jesse immediately prayed over Bear and that spirit of murder was gone.

When we got home that night, there were several messages on our answering machine. Several familiar voices said things like, "Bear, I hope it wasn't me you were mad at. I apologize if I made you mad..."

At the convention the next day, some people came up and gave us money. They, too, apologized and said, "I hope it wasn't me you were mad at. I'm sorry I didn't keep my word to you about giving to your ministry. Here's a start of my monthly giving."

When we got home that night, there was a whole set of nice living room furniture sitting in our carport. We still aren't sure where it came from. People from every direction wanted to make amends. We didn't know what they were apologizing for. The one that Bear was mad at, never apologized, but Bear was set free from the grudge and it never bothered him again.

Jesse and Cathy Duplantis with Dove and Bear at Words of Life Church in Miami, Florida.

Chapter 24
Miami

In the fear of the Lord is strong confidence: and his children shall have a place of refuge.

Proverbs 14:26

That fall, we had several invitations to come to minister in the state of Florida, so we spent some time in the Miami area. We were scheduled to preach at a neat Spanish speaking church, that was pastored by a sweet couple who treated us like royalty and

Dove and Bear preaching at The Christian Retreat in Florida.

put us up in a really nice condo. They shared with us about other guests that had slept in that same bed including Buddy and Pat Harrison, Kenneth Hagin's son-in-law and daughter. We were blessed and looking forward to the services the next day.

Before I went to sleep that night, I tucked Micah into her little bed in the other room, and then thought about the faith giants that had slept in that very bed that I was crawling into. I finally drifted off to sleep with Bear beside me. He had already been asleep for more than an hour. I never felt him get up, but Bear was awake by four in the morning. He crawled quietly out of bed to spend some time with the Lord. He wanted to be anointed to preach a special message to these people we had fallen in love with. Bear looked for his Bible and realized it was still in the van.

He snuck out quietly so he wouldn't bother Micah and I so early in the morning. After going out to the condo parking lot and getting his Bible out of the van, Bear made his way back to the big gate. It was then that he noticed the gate had locked behind him. There was a number code, but he had no idea what the code was. Here he was, wearing just a pair of shorts, no shirt, no shoes, tattoos all over his body, with a Bible under his arm, stuck outside a strange place at four o'clock in the morning. Bear's hair always stood on end when he woke up in the morning, too. He was thinking he would get in and out of the condo without seeing anyone at that time of day. All of a sudden, he knew he'd better start walking because he had to go to the bathroom, real bad.

As Bear walked along the sidewalk carrying his Bible, he noticed some groups of men that were circling him. They would get closer, point at him, and then take off running. He tried to ask a few people where a bathroom was, but they would say something in Spanish, turn and go the other way. Bear just kept walking, looking for a much needed bathroom by now. He finally saw a gas station up ahead.

Bear had to go in to get the key for the restroom to be opened. The man didn't speak English, but he quickly threw Bear the key. People were staring from all directions. When Bear gave the bathroom key back to the man in the gas station, he looked scared, and motioned for Bear to hurry and leave.

Finally Bear got back to the condo. By now it was around six o'clock. A lady came walking out of the condo and Bear grabbed the gate before it shut. He came back in and woke me up a little after six, telling me all about his adventure of being locked outside of the gate. I had no idea he was ever gone. Bear got some study time in before we left for the service. Before we knew it, we were all three dressed and heading out for church.

When we got to the church, Bear told his whole story to Pastor Angel. With a huge laugh, the pastor started telling us what a terrible neighborhood Bear walked through. He said it was filled with gangs and people are robbed nearly every day on those same streets. He told Bear how those men that were circling him had been gangs.

"But why did they run?" Bear asked.

"Because of all of your tattoos!" said Pastor Angel. He laughed as he told Bear how only the meanest men would have that many tattoos in their part of the world. "They thought you were loco, Brother Bear! A man with that many tattoos, with bare feet, no shirt, and a Bible under his arm. They surely thought you were loco!"

Chapter 25
The Car Hauler

Many are the afflictions of the righteous, But the Lord delivers him out of them all.

Psalm 34:19 (NKJV)

While we were on our way to preach in Tampa one time, we were driving our minivan that had nearly 200,000 miles on it. We believed God to get us everywhere we went.

On this trip the van had been acting up. Neither one of us were mechanics. Bear would look under the hood and wiggle wires hoping that something would help. I would ask people that were stopped at rest areas along the way if they could look under our hood and tell us what seemed to be the problem.

We needed to get to the Tampa area by that night to preach at a meeting the next morning and we were only able to go around 45 miles an hour. Finally something snapped under the hood and we limped into a rest stop that was just up ahead. We were right outside of Tallahassee.

Pretending to be mechanics again, we both had our heads under the hood trying to figure out the problem. In reality, we were both hoping it would draw some interest and someone would walk over to help. No one made the move to come over.

Then we saw a big car hauler drive up. He parked his rig, which was empty of any cars, and walked directly over to where we were parked.

"Have a problem?" the man asked with a sincere voice. We told him what it sounded like before we coasted in to the rest area.

"Well, I'm not a mechanic either. Where you goin'?" He quizzed.

"We have to be in the Tampa area to preach tomorrow morning."

The man looked at his car hauler rig and said, "Let's just hop your van on my hauler. I know a friend that's a mechanic in Tampa. I'll drop you off and let him fix your van, and you'll be where you need to be by morning. I'm heading to Tampa, also."

God was at work, as usual! We loaded the van and rode in the cab of the truck with the man. As we visited, he shared that he knew the Lord and had no reason to stop at that rest area. He just knew the Lord wanted him to. Micah and I took a nap in the sleeper as Bear shared his testimony with the driver. We were driving into Tampa before we knew it and the mechanic had just what was needed to fix the van. No one wanted any money and the part was all we had to pay for which was under $60. The next morning we preached at Billy Burke's church in Clearwater. We borrowed a Harley and were able to ride into the sanctuary. Bear shared his testimony and many came to the altar to receive prayer.

Chapter 26
Visited by an Angel

Are they not all ministering spirits, sent forth to minister for them who shall be heirs of salvation?

Hebrews 1:14

During our travels across the United States, we acquired several different motor homes. It was so nice to have our own home on wheels since we'd be out sometimes for as long as seven weeks at a time.

One particular time, Micah and I had to stay behind to do some local speaking, while Bear was invited to speak at some churches and prisons on the road for a week. Bear called me from Alabama and was in a daze about what had just happened to him. With a shaky voice he told me that he had been driving the motor home, listening to the song, *Yes, Lord, We will Ride.*

"Baby, an angel visited me in the motor home!"

"Really!" I exclaimed. "Tell me what happened!"

"I was singing along with the music tape and all of a sudden I felt such a holy presence that I had to pull the motor home over and pull into a rest stop," Bear spoke in a solemn manner from his heart. "The presence was so strong; there was a literal weight in the atmosphere. I couldn't sit up. I had to lay down on the couch behind the driver's seat."

"Then an angel appeared. It wasn't a little angel; it was a *huge man angel*." Bear continued. "And he stood right over me and touched my lips with his sword." As Bear finished, he was crying. "I'll never forget the way *he looked me in the eyes*."

Bear finished his story with, "I don't know why it happened to ME, but I do know there was a special anointing that was left. I sense a *fresh new ability to speak the Word of God like I never had before*."

As Bear shared the event with me, I knew it had been a holy time and I could sense the anointing even through the phone.

From then on Bear did have a fresh anointing, with a new boldness and ability to speak the Word like never before.

Bear praying for prisoners in Brazil.

Bear teaching in Kisumu, Kenya, East Africa.

Bear preaching in East Africa at the Jerry Savelle Revival Fires Conference.

Chapter 27
On the Road Again

**But you be watchful in all things, endure afflictions,
do the work of an evangelist, fulfill your ministry.**
2 Timothy 4:5 (NKJV)

One time during the summer, we were heading to preach at a prison in Ohio and then on to minister in some churches. We stopped to take Micah to the *Precious Moments* property just north of Joplin, Missouri, near Carthage. We'd been there before, but Bear thought Micah would enjoy it more now that she was getting older.

By the time we left the *Precious Moments* grounds, we realized we really had some miles to put on to get where we were going. Bear liked to drive all night as long as he had some coffee to stay awake. It looked like an all nighter was in the works.

When we got to the border of Ohio, Bear was really tired. It was hot and he liked to hang his arm out of the window as he drove along. His hair was long, and the wind had whipped it most of the night. He hadn't shaved for a few days, and was looking a bit scraggly. It was around 2 o'clock in the afternoon by now and we still had a couple hours to go to get to our destination. We were driving on the freeway, and Bear was pushing the speed limit a bit too much. We saw a policeman turn his lights on right behind us. Bear found a place to pull over. The officer went to Bear's window and said he wanted him out of the vehicle. Bear got out and stood in front of the officer.

Bear was so tired, he couldn't remember where his wallet was. The officer was asking questions outside of the motor home and I could hear what was being said. The officer said that they were looking for a motor home that was packing drugs and the driver's description fit Bear to a tee. Bear was answering the questions all wrong. When the officer asked Bear where he was going, Bear stated clearly the answer, "To prison."

"I'm sure you are," the policeman assured him. The officer told Bear he was going to have to take him in to jail if he didn't show his driver's license. We found it, and the officer still had lots of questions. Then he brought out a drug dog and said he had to search our motor home. The entire time this was going on, Micah sat at our little table calmly and colored a picture with her crayons. She looked up at me from her artwork and said in her little voice, "I don't think the policeman likes Daddy, but he'll feel better when I give him this picture I made." After what seemed an eternity, the officer let Bear go. He poked his head into the motor home to say goodbye and said he was sorry to inconvenience us. Micah handed him her drawing and Bear handed him his testimony on tape. The officer turned out to be a Christian. We were so glad to finally pull away and get back on the road again.

Chapter 28
Our Home on Wheels

...But as for me and my house, we will serve the Lord.

Joshua 24:15

Another trip in the motor home, we were heading to Tampa again. We were coming along that stretch about 50 miles west of Tallahassee, heading east. We had some praise music playing loud and we were singing along with the tape. Suddenly, Bear saw smoke out of his rearview mirror. He looked again, and it was gone. It was a very hot summer day and as usual, we had some miles to put on to get to where we were going. Bear shrugged it off, thinking it was just the heat bouncing off of the freeway.

We kept singing with the music, when finally another car drove up next to us honking and waving. Bear rolled his window down to see what they wanted.

"Your motor home is on fire!" The people yelled out their car window pointing down.

Bear steered the motor home to the right and we parked it as soon as we could. We were both shouting prayers in the name of Jesus. We hopped out of the motor home to find the flames were shooting out pretty good. It had even started a couple grass fires on the side of the freeway. We got a fire extinguisher out of the motor home and stopped the fire under the engine. We felt helpless to stop the grass fires because they were spreading fast. Within five minutes, a fire truck showed up from nowhere. He was able to put out the grassfires and look at our motor home. As he searched it out, the fireman couldn't even find anything. It was like it never happened. We hit the road again and the motor home never got hot again.

A few years later, we were going through Little Rock, Arkansas and had planned to attend Happy Caldwell's mission conference while we passed through the state. Our motor home had been running just fine, but as soon as we got a mile or so from Agapé Church, a pin in the steering column broke and we were unable to go forward. Bear coasted back down the hill and parked it. He thought he would just walk up and get help at the church, while Micah and I waited behind. A police officer arrived and directed traffic around us since we were parked in the middle of the road. Finally a guy from the church brought Bear back. They looked under the hood and decided that we would have to be towed in to a mechanic. They gave us the number of a tow truck they knew. Bear said he would wait for the tow truck to come, and Micah and I could go to the church since the meetings were about to start. Bear said there was no sense in all three of us missing out on the teachings for that session. So the man from church took Micah and I back to Agapé.

Soon the tow truck showed up with Bear and the police officer standing near the motor home. The young man that drove the tow truck, seemed a bit confused. Bear said he was stunned as he watched that young man hook up to our motor home and back it over a brick mailbox that was on the edge of the street. Then he pulled it off the mailbox ripping the floor out near the entrance door. He then rehooked it from the side and pulled it nearly apart. Then he towed it to the church parking lot. Bear was in shock. He was trying not to be too upset, but he and the tow truck driver had a few words. I was so glad the old Bear was no longer there or fists would be flying. The police officer said she would be glad to be a witness to what happened. The insurance company showed up at the church the next day and declared our motor home was totaled. It had been our home on wheels for a couple of years so we had much of our belongings in it.

Happy and Jeanie Caldwell were so good to us. While we had to wait for the insurance paperwork to be finished, they put us up in a motel nearby and gave us money for food. We were able to attend all of the mission conference, and had to stay a few extra days. We decided that I would rent a small U-Haul truck and clean out the motor home, while Bear rented a car and kept going to keep the speaking engagements. Micah and I would go back to Texas with our goods, and Bear would be home in a couple weeks. We weren't exactly excited about the plan, but we knew it would have to work this time. We were just thankful for the provision of the Lord and knew He was still on the throne.

Chapter 29
Dove's Harley

Therefore I say to you, whatever things you ask when you pray, believe that you receive them, and you will have them.

Mark 11:24 (NKJV)

As the ministry grew, we rented office space in town. First it was one office, then a second, and finally we had three spaces in the same strip mall in Crowley, Texas. God was blessing Loving Hearts Ministry and we were getting calls to preach all over the world. Bear was never supposed to leave the U.S. according to his prison release papers. One morning he got up and informed me the Lord had spoken to him to go and apply for a passport. He did and within four weeks he had it back. There was nothing stopping Bear when he knew God wanted him to do something. He loved to travel no matter where in the world it was.

Bear's first love of travel was to ride his motorcycle. After having one for a couple years, he thought I should get a Harley, too. "I'm going to believe for you to get your own Harley someday. You deserve it," he would say every few weeks. I thought it would be nice, but I was plenty busy with the needs of the ministry and didn't think about it a whole lot. I had borrowed a little Honda for awhile just to practice on so I would be ready in case a bike came along.

One day we were attending Brother Jerry Savelle's Revival Fires meetings. He had it in a big tent at his ministry grounds that year. Bear leaned over to me and said I want to plant seed into a bike for you." I handed him the checkbook and thought it was a sweet gesture. Just as they were receiving the offering, Brother Jerry's pilot flew his plane over the tent. It was amazingly loud. I heard a Harley in the spirit right then. Others said they heard their own planes, I heard my own Harley.

That night, we were back at the meetings. Before the service started, I got a message from one of the workers that Brother Jerry along with Dick Rueben, wanted to see me. We made our way to the meeting room where the men were waiting. I had no idea what they wanted me for.

"Dove, the Lord told me today to give you my bike," Dick said clearly. I was silent and it just didn't register in my brain for a few minutes.

"It's like a custom low rider," he went on to say. "It's got the *evo engine* with *Edelbrock high performance heads*. It's on a *Paugho frame* and it's a *good looking bike*. I knew when I got it that it would belong to someone else. I know I'm supposed to plant it into your life."

It was so exciting to think about me having my own bike that I couldn't sleep that night. The bike was still at Dick's place in Indiana, but a friend from Fort Worth, Charlie Tackett, met him halfway to pick the bike up for me a month or so later.

When our friend helped me unload my new bike, I wanted to sleep with it that night! I was glad that it fit right into the back door in our house. I wiped it down, checked bolts, and tightened everything there was to tighten! It took me a couple days to get used to the weight of my new ride. Finally, I was going down the freeway on my own bike with Bear in front of me on his.

Chapter 30
The Bike Trip to Montana

Cast not away your confidence, which has great recompense of reward.
Hebrews 10:35

Brother Jerry started the *Chariots of Light motorcycle club*, and planned some trips around the country. I heard about the Montana run that was coming up and told Bear I wanted to go. It was to end up in Kalispell and sounded like a great trip to me.

He was all for it so we had a friend come over and do a check-up on my bike, making sure it was road worthy. I got a *Clymer Manual* to study so I could wrench on my own scooter if I needed to. A biker brother had put a tool pouch together for me. We packed up what we could, making sure I had my tools and manual even if nothing else fit in!

It was so hot in Texas after we started out, that we had to pull over and rest in some shade. We decided to travel at night until we got out of the scorching heat. We'd ride as far as we could then stop and sleep on the side of the road. If it was too hot to sleep outside, we'd find a fast food restaurant and nap in a corner. Once I woke up in a Wendy's to find little faces staring at me. We had a long ride ahead and tried to stay up on our rest for our own safety. Running into a couple rain storms in Texas caused us to have to wait a few extra hours under a gas station overhang. We were still making pretty good time considering the elements.

We did good getting to Colorado, and then my bike started having a few challenges. The battery seemed to be the problem and Bear was getting tired of pushing me to get it started. Several times things quit working, but I studied my *Clymer Manual* on the side of the road and figured it out myself almost every time. Once while we were still in Colorado, my bike just quit going down the road. A farmer was going by with an empty flatbed trailer and he stopped to see if we needed anything.

"We need to get to a Harley shop," Bear told him. I knew if I could get to a shop they could help confirm what the problem was. I thought it was the *voltage regulator*.

"The nearest Harley shop is only ten miles away," the man said.

I asked the farmer if he thought he could take us. He said he didn't have anything to tie the bike down with.

"I'll just sit on it while you haul it," I told him, knowing we had to do something.

The farmer reluctantly agreed and we loaded the bike. I hopped on holding it up just like we were going down the road on our own. Bear followed right behind on his Harley. It was the quietest ride that Harley had ever given me!

When we got to the Harley shop, sure enough their mechanic agreed with me. He had the new part, but no time to put it in. He was backed up with a line of folks waiting.

"I'll do it myself," I told him. I pulled out my manual, and before we knew it, I fired her up and we were ready to hit the road again.

Chapter 31
Outlaw Friends

For God sent not His Son into the world to condemn the world; but that the world through Him might be saved.

John 3:17

As we crossed the state of Wyoming, the wind blew hard. My arms got so tired of holding the bike up against the 50 to 70 mile an hour wind gusts. Several people asked me if my rear got tired on the trip. I had to say "no, it wasn't my rear it was my arms." Sometimes I would get blown to the other lane of the highway. One time we pulled over and I parked my bike on the road side to walk back and talk to Bear. My bike was leaning on the kickstand and looked fine. I looked up a minute later and the wind had blown it over — on the opposite side of the kickstand. The wind was the strongest I had ever seen. I was glad there wasn't much traffic on the road we were on. *I prayed all the time.*

At one of our fuel stops, we pulled into the gas station and saw some bikers working on a trike. It was owned by one of their patch holders. One of them walked over to us and asked if we had any tools. I said I did, and that they were welcome to anything we had. I handed one of them my leather pouch of tools so they could look at what was in it.

"There it is! Just what we need," he said as he pulled out my 13/16" spark plug socket. Bear and I parked our bikes after we gassed up and sat down on the ground by the trike getting worked on. The bikers were all part of an *outlaw club* that was from Denver. They were heading to Sturgis. They generously offered us coffee and snacks. As we visited, Bear shared parts of his testimony with them.

"I've heard of you," one guy said. "One of our club brothers served time with you a long time ago. He told us all about it." As Bear talked to them, he found out that he had served time with one of their club brothers. It was years ago and Bear always wondered where the guy ended up. All of the men shared war stories, bike

wrecks and trips they remembered. Bear shared with them all about how he had been saved in prison, walked with Jesus now and lived a different way of life. We sat and visited with them for an hour or two while they worked on the trike and got it ready to get back on the road again. Finally, it was done. We said our goodbyes and the president handed us his card.

"Any time you're in Denver, look me up. You're welcome to stay at the clubhouse anytime. And if you ever need anything, we're here for you." We knew we had some *covenant friends* now in Denver. As we pulled away on our bikes, I looked back at the new outlaw brothers and they were all standing there, waving good-bye. One of them yelled, "Keep 'em up!" referring to our bikes staying safe on the road. There was a sort of sadness in my heart that we needed to spend more time with them. As we cranked our Harley's up the hill from the gas station, I asked the Lord to send *more laborers into that harvest*. Those guys were *special to my heart* already.

After another day of riding, we finally made it to Kalispell, Montana and joined Brother Jerry. It had taken us five days to go over 1600 miles. With a few breakdowns, lots of pushing my bike, and many stories to share, we had finally arrived. Boy, were we glad.

Chapter 32
Air Life

I had fainted, unless I had believed to see the goodness of the Lord in the land of the living.

Psalm 27:13

The very next year, Bear wanted to go on Brother Jerry's Montana run again. We were scheduled to be at Ellson Bennett's meeting, *The Healing of the Nations*, in Kayenta, Arizona a week later. Bear was one of the guest speakers, as well as Brother Copeland. I decided to stay behind since I was committed to hauling some supplies out for Ellson to use on the reservation. So Bear and a friend took off on their bikes, heading to Montana. They would ride to Montana and then down to Arizona where they would meet me by the time *The Healing of the Nations* meetings started. Micah and I began loading the cargo trailer, as she and I would drive our red dually pulling the trailer full of my bike, and things we were giving to Ellson.

A couple days after Bear arrived in Montana, I got a phone call in the evening. It was from a man that worked for Jerry Savelle.

"Dove," he said slowly. "Bear had an accident on his bike and just got on an air life helicopter. We think he has a broken neck. We're believing God for his healing. Brother Jerry wanted me to let you know..." As I got off the phone, I was totally stunned. I wanted to cry, but I knew I had to be strong. Bear had hit a pothole in the road and went down an embankment while they were riding through Yellowstone. The bike flipped over and landed on top of him. People that witnessed the accident thought surely it had killed him.

Micah came into the room and asked what was wrong. I shared with her what had just transpired on the phone and she ran to the other room in tears.

"We have to be strong for Daddy, Honey. Come back here and let's pray." As I held her in my arms, the Lord told me we had to take communion right then. We received the elements and declared Bear was healed and whole. We shouted from the Word of God that Micah's daddy would *live and not die* and that he would *declare the goodness of God in the land of the living*. Micah ran and got the shofar we had on a shelf in our living room. She blew it as best she could, knowing it was the sound of victory. I knew I couldn't just tell anyone about Bear unless they were strong in faith. I only felt comfortable in calling a couple friends to pray. The first one I called was my friend, Vikki Burke. Vikki immediately agreed with me in prayer and spoke only faith and life to the situation. I was blessed to share the burden with her. Pastor George and Terri, from Eagle Mountain Church, offered to buy my airplane ticket to Salt Lake City, where Bear was hospitalized. The following day, I was on a plane heading to Utah.

As I sat among the people on the plane, I knew I couldn't share with anyone why I was traveling or fear would be released. The lady next to me wanted to chat. When she asked my reason for the flight, I just said I was going to meet my husband. "Business or pleasure?" she asked. I told her it was business. I told myself that was true since we seriously believed God for a miracle. *I was all business.* Little did she know how I shook inside and *hung on to the promises of God with all my might.*

Chapter 33
At the Hospital

He sent His word, and healed them, and delivered them from their destructions.

Psalm 107:20

I finally arrived at the Salt Lake airport. I had called a partner of Loving Hearts Ministry, Suki Brown, and she offered to pick me up and let me stay at her house.

Suki met me at the airport and we quickly made our way to the hospital. Finding Bear's room, I walked in. He was laying in a bed with his neck in a huge brace. He was *smiling and sharing Jesus* with all of the hospital staff. One of the nurses was testing his legs and feet to see if he had any feeling.

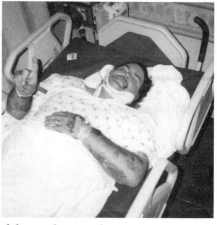

Bear shouted for joy when he saw me come in. He knew I'd get there as fast as I could. After several hugs and hellos, Bear told me the *good report*.

"It's coming back," Bear grinned. "I couldn't feel a thing earlier today, but *now I can feel my legs* a little when they touch me!"

"He's a miracle man," one of the nurses said. "We've seen this kind of an accident before and *no one has come out without some paralyzation.*"

The doctor came in and shared with us how Bear had a *very serious break in his neck.* He said usually a man would have been killed or at least in a wheelchair for the rest of their life. It was a *very similar break as what Christopher Reeves had.* He said all Bear would have to do is to *wear a metal "halo" for a couple months.* It was a big metal contraption that had to be screwed into Bear's skull. It sounded kind of bad, but it was much better than not being able to walk again. *We rejoiced in God's goodness.*

After the halo was on, the doctor informed Bear that he would need to stay at the hospital for several weeks. The doctor also mentioned that they *spotted a small tumor* in Bear's head in the x-rays they had taken for the broken neck. But when they found out we had no insurance, they never mentioned it again.

"I've got to get to Kayenta," Bear said to the doctor. "*I have a promise to keep* that I would be there. My brother is counting on me." Bear had made the commitment to Ellson months before. As soon as Bear wanted to leave, they said he could.

Four days later, Bear walked out of that hospital on his own two feet. He even ministered at a church that night and several people were touched and changed forever.

Chapter 34
The Healing of the Nations

...for the healing of the nations. And there shall be no more curse....
Revelation 22:2,3

I had gone back to Texas on a flight as soon as the halo was placed on Bear's head.

Back in Texas, Micah and I loaded the trailer, hooked up the red dually and then headed to Kayenta. Her little dachshund puppy, Sam, was our only other passenger.

Kenneth Copeland had offered to fly Bear from Salt Lake City to Kayenta, in his plane with his pilot. Bear was ecstatic that he was going to make it to the *Healing of the Nations* after all.

As I was driving from Crowley to Kayenta, I had a *visitation* from the Spirit of God. At that time, we still only had two office spaces in the strip mall in Crowley for Loving Hearts Ministry. The Lord spoke to me that we were to rent a third office space in our strip mall. He showed me that it would begin a meeting place, filled with people, and that it would be the *beginning of a*

church. For hours, I even rehearsed some of the things I would teach on. I was so excited it helped me drive straight through that 24 hour trek.

Micah and I finally arrived in Kayenta, and that same afternoon Bear flew in to the reservation landing strip. It had been *one week* since the accident at Yellowstone. They had to work at getting Bear to fit in the seat of the plane with that big metal halo connected to him. He said he had a great flight, but had to look up at the ceiling the whole trip. He was *smiling ear to ear*, though,

just to have made it in time to preach. He was scheduled to speak that night.

The meeting was held outdoors in the arena at the fairgrounds. It was a warm August night and the crowd kept coming in. Praise

Bear with halo neck brace and Kenneth Copeland at the Healing of the Nations meeting.

and worship was very anointed that night as Jonathan Maracle played and sang the song *Rise Up Mighty Warrior*. People everywhere danced to the music in their native attire. *Bear joined them, halo and all*.

When it was his time to preach, Bear spoke with all of his heart about the Blood of Jesus. Someone brought up a chair for him to use, but he stood to preach anyway. He didn't seem to be hindered at all by the big metal halo bolted to his head. He made a call for those that wanted to come for prayer and the altar was full. Then Ellson shared that *Bear was a true warrior* for making it to the meeting no matter what it took. *Bear knew he had to keep his word to his Native American brother no matter what.*

After we got back to Texas, Bear went to the doctor in Fort Worth and immediately the doctor was upset as he looked at the halo. He informed us it had been *put on wrong* and Bear *could have been paralyzed at any time.* He made an emergency appointment for Bear to get right in and have it redone. We were so thankful that even though the halo had been put on wrong, it had *not left any damage.*

A local lawyer heard the story about the halo that was put on wrong and wanted to take the case. He told Bear to accept that he would never be the same because of the negligence of the other hospital. Bear got mad at the lawyer and told him to leave.

"If you're telling me I'll have to say I'm hurt and not healed just to make a point, I don't want anything to do with you. *Jesus is my lawyer and He says I'm healed and whole.*" And Bear was. The halo came off after a few more weeks and *Bear was able to resume life as usual.* A few times *I wondered about the tumor* the Utah hospital had found, but *we just shrugged it off knowing our God was in charge.*

Chapter 35
Eagle's Rest

But they that wait upon the LORD shall renew their strength; they shall mount up with wings as eagles; they shall run, and not be weary; and they shall walk, and not faint.

Isaiah 40:31

As the ministry grew, many parolees were showing up at the Loving Hearts building with needs for food, clothing and counseling. Bear and I were always busy helping them plug into jobs, churches and help them with food from our food pantry. Finally, the Lord spoke to us to start a *support group meeting* for those that had served time, lived on the streets or just wanted freedom from the bondage of drugs and alcohol.

We announced our first meetings to be held on Tuesday nights at one of the ministry offices in Crowley. It was to be called *Eagle's Rest*, a place where *eagles could fly in and rest*. We knew the folks we were called to could relate to the eagle. We  wanted it to be a setting where everyone felt *love, acceptance and forgiveness*. It grew from five people the first night, to over 50 in two months. We rented the Crowley Park meeting hall and held a special *free Thanksgiving dinner just for those that had served time and their families.* A sponsor donated all of the food from a local restaurant. Over 100 people came. We awarded special trophies and eagles to those that had been out the longest or that had the best success story and small eagles to everyone that had served any time at all. It was a very special night of love and hope. All of our Board of Directors showed up and we had planned to meet at the Loving Hearts office after the dinner was over. Soon we were sitting in the Eagle's Rest meeting room where Bear and I shared our hearts. "We believe we're supposed to *start a church for our people,*" Bear began. "Nearly all of them don't go to church anywhere and they say the Tuesday night Eagle's Rest meetings are their church. What do you all think?"

It was unanimous. The Board knew we should start a church. That very week God brought us a praise team and the building to meet in.

A special musical couple, Brian and Nancy Haralson who we met a few weeks earlier, said they'd be glad to do the music. They were very anointed musicians. We knew our people would love their style.

Loving Hearts Ministry Building in Crowley, Texas.

Bear asked if we could use the Crowley Moose Lodge for our church services and right away they got behind us. We met at two o'clock in the afternoon on Sunday since *most of our folks liked to sleep in*. Soon after a couple weeks, the church was growing and God was moving in a mighty way. Within our first year, we had over 65 people saved and many baptized in water.

One of the outreaches we did as a church, we called *Drive By Blessings*. Many of our congregation had been involved with drive by shootings, but now had given their lives to Jesus. God gave me an idea that we could drive by and bless families with a big box filled with a Christmas dinner — including a turkey or ham, and gifts for each member of the family. We had many low income families sign up with an application we called a *green sheet*. It was a big project, but we did it. *Eagle Mountain church sent a team to help us and hundreds of families in the rough parts of Fort Worth and Dallas were blessed each Christmas.*

Chapter 36
The Men's Home

God makes a home for the lonely; He leads out the
prisoners into prosperity....
                              Psalm 68:6 (NASB)

The same month we started the church, we also rented
the house next door to help people out. We saw
such a huge need to house men coming out of prison or
off the streets. We knew our own house couldn't hold
them all and we wanted to do more. We knew we
*couldn't complain about the need unless we were willing to do
something about it.* So we did our best to make a difference in men that needed a new start.

Soon there were men coming in from all over the
United States to get into our men's home. Some had
served time in prison, some lived on the street, and
some had drug and alcohol problems. Several had to
kick hard drugs in the home; some had blue warrants
out for their arrest. *All needed a fresh start.*

Bear held the men's home with very high regard.
Each man that came in was just as important as the last
one. Bear was a true example of *bearing one another's bur-
dens and so fulfill the law of Christ.* Anytime the men
needed anything, we did our best to make it happen.

One day one of the men got a call that his grand-
mother in North Dakota had passed away. That night
Bear decided to take him all the way to North Dakota

where the funeral was to be held in two days. They drove all night, the next day, and the next night to make it thirty minutes before the funeral was to begin. *Bear constantly showed what covenant was about* and the men's home guys *knew we had their back.*

We had very little funding for the men's home so we taught them how to believe God for themselves. Sometimes we would have as many as fifteen men in the home at one time. Many would need clothes, glasses, dental work and shoes. Food would show up, beds were given, clothes would come in, and even several sides of beef were donated right when it was needed the most. One of our men needed dentures and a woman out of state donated the money for him to get them. The local dentist and beauty parlor were always giving low cost services to our men. *They saw the favor and provision of the Lord at all times.* Faith came by hearing the Word every day.

One time a partner donated enough money that was designated to take all thirteen men out to an exceptionally nice restaurant. We were so proud of them and showed them off as we acted like *mom and dad* to men that varied in ages from eighteen to sixty, all colors and sizes. They all dressed up in their finest clothes, with some having to borrow from one another. It was fun as many of them had never seen a menu with meals including Mahi Mahi fish on it or ordered a real sirloin steak. It was an evening I'm sure they'll always remember. I know I always will.

The men had Bible and life skill classes in the morning and did work around the home or ministry in the afternoon. Then evenings were spent going to meetings or doing Bible study in the men's home. Even without the funding to have a proper director, we watched the men grow in faith and trust more in God. Although, we did have plenty of challenges as well. Several times our ministry van was stolen, sold for crack cocaine and we had to go find it on the south side of Fort Worth. Sometimes we had drug dealers at the door trying to peddle their goods to our men. Sometimes our lawn care equipment ended up at the local pawn shop. Once a guy came in that was so high, he ended up tackling several police all at the same time.

Most of them did want the Lord and we were amazed at the way they prayed for one another. We knew *we were building an army* and I was always so proud of the men. They were one big family to us and we loved them all. These pages couldn't hold all of the stories that could be told about the 126 men that came through the home within the four years we had it operating.

Bear with the men from the men's home.

Chapter 37
The Diagnosis

Behold, I will bring it health and cure, and I will cure them, and will reveal unto them the abundance of peace and truth.

Jeremiah 33:6

In the summer of 2002, I noticed Bear was beginning to sleep more and seemed to have a headache often. While riding the bike with him to Kayenta, Arizona that summer, I noticed some of his decisions in traffic were not safe. When we made it to Kayenta to join Ellson again at the Healing of the Nations, Bear sat on the edge of our bed at the motel and said he felt something was about to change in our ministry. I remember thinking at the time that I'd never seen him act like that before. I finally talked him into getting a physical and complete check over by a doctor friend that had been a student at J.S.M.I. Bear reluctantly agreed and went to see the doctor and had a professional cat scan at a nearby facility.

A few days later, the doctor called. The diagnosis wasn't good. The x-rays they took showed a huge brain stem tumor, already the size of a small potato. In the natural, they said Bear only had a few weeks to live. We were devastated, but as always, hung on to each other and to the promises of God.

"I'm not ready to die. It's not my time yet." Bear said in a determined voice. I knew his faith was always stronger than anything the devil had thrown our way. But this time, my faith was a bit shaky.

He assured me each day. "I'm gonna live and not die!" Bear would say as he listened to the Kenneth Copeland Healing music CD. He worked on making sure his diet was extremely healthy. There were others that shared healthy ways to combat tumors and brought us their products. It seemed to be working. Bear was not having the headaches any more and he had new-found energy. We were certain the tumor was shrinking.

He was feeling so good the spring of 2003, that he wanted us to both ride our bikes to the *Thunder Over Texas* motorcycle rally north of Fort Worth. Bear had a great time that day and entered his bike in the People's Choice contest. He was so excited when it was announced that his bike won. What a special day the Lord blessed us with. Bear was determined he would live a long life on the earth. Little did I know then that *things were about to change.*

Chapter 38
Heaven's Music

And I saw a new Heaven and a new earth...and there shall be no more death, neither sorrow, nor crying....

Revelation 21:1,4

We really believed with all of our hearts that Bear's healing had come. He was driving again and sleeping without any pain medication. The power of God was present to heal and we knew it was happening to Bear.

Then one day, Bear and I were outside and he looked at me and said, "Did you hear that?"

"Hear what?" I asked not knowing what he was talking about.

"The music!" Bear said like he was aggravated with me for not hearing it. He described it to be the most beautiful music he'd ever heard.

"I can get closer to it if I want to," he explained. I still didn't hear a thing. Nothing was said about it until a few weeks went by.

"There it is! The music! Don't you hear it this time?" Bear quizzed me again. I still didn't hear it. What was he talking about? Bear shared with me again how beautiful it was and how *he wanted to get closer so he could hear it better*.

"I can get closer to it if I want to, but I don't want to leave you." Bear stated plainly. I didn't know what he meant, but he was so sure of himself, *I didn't want to ask.*

A few weeks later, Bear came home from church one evening in excruciating pain. He opened the front door of our home and could barely walk up the steps to our bedroom. His whole body shook with convulsions and he said he was freezing. I called for an ambulance. When the ambulance got there, Micah stayed out on the porch crying. The neighbors came over to try to comfort her. Everyone on our street was there to help. The ambulance driver tried to console Micah and told her that her daddy just had the flu. Micah knew better. She yelled at him that he didn't know what he was talking about.

"My daddy doesn't have the flu! *He's dying!!!*" Micah screamed into the night. It was a dark hour for all of us. It seemed like a bad dream and surely I would wake up anytime now. I quoted healing scriptures all the way to the hospital.

When we got to the hospital, Bear was admitted to a room in the emergency ward. *He asked if I heard the music again.* I still couldn't hear it.

"I want to go there," he said. *"It's full of light and the most beautiful place I've ever seen.* It's so much different than here." I knew Bear must have seen Heaven.

I argued with him in tears as we waited for the doctor to see him.

"You can't leave me here! We're covenant! We're back to back!" my heart was pounding as I let him know how I felt. I felt like I was sinking. I grabbed his hands in that hospital bed and spoke the Word of God to him quoting all the scriptures I knew.

"It's so bright there, too. *I want to go, but not yet...*"
Bear said as he was drifting off to sleep. The nurse had
just come by and given him something for the pain.

Questions raced through my mind. What about the
healing power of God? Why was Bear talking about going somewhere? What would Micah and I do if he did
go? The ministry needed him. How could I run Loving
Hearts without him? The names Bear and Dove went together. No, it was too much to think about. Surely he
would stand for his healing and stay here with us.

Chapter 39
A Promise Kept

For I am persuaded, that neither death, nor life, nor angels, nor principalities, nor powers, nor things present, nor things to come,

Nor height, nor depth, nor any other creature, shall be able to separate us from the love of God, which is in Christ Jesus our Lord.

Romans 8:38,39

Bear ended up in the hospital again several times. He talked about the music, but said *he still wasn't ready to go.* One time when he was in the hospital, it looked as if he was choosing Heaven for sure. The doctors came in and said it could be that Bear would not make it past the night. He was having trouble breathing and seemed to be slipping away.

All of the family — Riley with his fiancé, Nikki, and Ty and his wife, Rachel, and Lain were in Bear's hospital room and he was asleep. As we sat and watched him, his breathing became sporadic and labored. We all sat on the edge of his bed and cried as we thought we were watching Bear pass over to the other side. Rachel, being the nurse of the family, shared with us about what were normal symptoms as a person was about to go to Heaven. The dreaded *death rattle* was evident. We were all bracing ourselves.

All of a sudden, *Bear's eyes popped open and he sat up in bed.*

"I've gotta go to the bathroom!" He exclaimed. We all helped him get up to go. When he came back to his bed, he started talking about how *he still had to go to the Healing of the Nations meetings* that were coming up soon.

"I promised Ellson I'd be there," Bear said as he laid his head back on his pillow. And somehow I knew he would keep that promise once again.

Several weeks passed and Bear was ready to go to the Healing of the Nations meetings. Brother Copeland offered to fly us in his plane so we could get there more comfortably. We had another anointed time and *Bear had kept his word.* On the flight home from Kayenta, Bear

Bear and Ellson Bennett.

spoke to me softly. We were looking out of the airplane window agreeing about the beautiful scenery when Bear turned to me with a serious look on his face.

"This is my last meeting," he said. "I'm going to tell the church that *I'm going to Heaven soon. It's just about time to go now.*" I was stunned by his words, but knew he meant what he said. I couldn't hold back the tears as Bear held my hand.

Several of our friends tried to talk Bear out of going to Heaven, but his mind was made up. I was upset with him for awhile. Finally Brother Copeland and a few others told me we had to release him and let him go. It was a Sunday service when he stood up in front of the congregation at Eagle's Rest and shared his heart.

"*This will be my last service here,*" Bear said bluntly. Folks throughout the congregation started crying. Several got up and went to the restroom.

"But don't be sad. *I'm going to a wonderful place* and I'll see you again. *I want to go.*"

After church, we had planned an ice cream feed. Bear joined in with a glad heart. He acted like he was *excited about his future.* Many of the people didn't know how to respond, but they all came up to Bear and told him how much they loved him and thanked him for being the great example and friend that he was.

Twenty minutes after Bear had gone to sleep that night, he came up out of our bed. Staggering and holding his head with both hands, he told me to call a nurse. He said something happened in his head and he knew he needed help. A nurse came right out to the house. By the time she was ready to leave, she had scheduled him to check into the hospice house in Fort Worth the next morning. I had no idea he *only had three weeks left on earth.*

Chapter 40
Hospice House

Even though I walk through the valley of the shadow of death, I will fear no evil, for you are with me....

Psalm 23:4 (NIV)

When Bear got checked in, he was still walking and didn't look like a person that would need hospice care. He was determined that he was heading home to Heaven, though, and shared that with everyone who came to see him. He enjoyed playing "Scrabble" and working with a puzzle in the lobby the first couple days.

One day after Bear had been there a week or so, his hospice doctor came in to see him.

"So how are you feeling, Mr. Morgan?" she asked.

"I'm doing great. I'm going home soon!" Bear shared excitedly.

He looked so good, the doctor went to the office and started filling out his release papers. She thought he meant he was going back to his house. She had no idea *he meant Heaven.* The workers on duty told her what Bear was really talking about. They let him stay because he still fit the criteria to be a hospice patient.

Bear told me to call everyone I could and invite them to come visit him.

"I'm not going to be here much longer so I want to see everyone I can," Bear said.

Within five days he had over 200 visitors, from bikers to businessmen and tattoos to purple hair. All of them were precious friends from all walks of life. Friends that couldn't come to Fort Worth called from around the world.

Mylon and Christi Le Fevre led singing one night when his room was full of people. Dennis O'Neill came and video taped Bear's farewell speech. Bear wanted it shown at his memorial. He also shared on tape how he wanted people to party at his home going and to serve all the banana splits and root beer floats that everyone could eat.

One day when Bear had a few visitors, he had dozed off and napped for a half hour or so. When he woke up, he sounded upset. I was right by his bedside trying to figure out what he meant.

"Someone in here wilted my flowers!" Bear was motioning to the flowers that were on top of the entertainment center in his room. They looked just fine to me, but he was seeing into the spirit.

"Who wilted my flowers?" Bear said again, this time with more volume. "I need everyone to leave except Dove and you," Bear pointed at a pastor that was in the room that had come to visit. He also invited Dennis and Vikki Burke to stay in the room and help him pray. Quickly everyone else left the room.

"You have a suicidal spirit on you," Bear said as he looked at the pastor. "You were thinking of killing yourself." Bear was speaking under the anointing and everyone was quiet. The pastor hung his head.

"I thought of it on my way here to see you, Bear." The pastor admitted he needed help so all of us joined

Bear in a powerful time of prayer, right there as Bear was in his hospice bed. A few minutes after praying, hugging the pastor and inviting the visitors back in, Bear looked up at the flowers. "Now they're back to normal," Bear said relieved. I still never saw a difference, but Bear was seeing into the supernatural realm.

Bear looked up and said, *"Isn't it amazing that a dying man can minister to a dead man and bring him life?"* Bear had no fear of death and sat with great wisdom in those last days on earth. *He seemed as excited to go to Heaven as someone would be if they got to go on a cruise or if* Dove with Bear at the hospice house *a child knew they were going to Disneyland.*

There were others that Bear had to call and said he needed to apologize to them. Sometimes he would suddenly ask me to call a certain person. He would get on the phone and prophesy over them. *Bear literally poured himself out during those three weeks he lived at hospice.* Finally, he knew his journey was almost complete.

Chapter 41
Travail

Never again will you be called the Godforsaken City or the Desolate Land. Your new name will be the City of God's Delight and the Bride of God, for the LORD delights in you and will claim you as his own.

Isaiah 62:4 (NLT)

Shortly before Bear went home to Heaven, I was talking to Pastor Allen Shook as he came to visit Bear. We were standing in the lobby at the hospice house. Pastor Allen was sharing with me how hard it was after his wife Beverly passed away; how he felt a literal hole inside him for a long time.

"I just wish there was a way to get rid of the wound you feel when a spouse goes to Heaven," Pastor Allen explained. He had since married again and said it finally was healed, but seems to be such a huge gaping wound at the time. I remember thinking as I listened to Pastor Allen, "Lord, help it not to be like that. Help heal my heart as Bear goes home to be with you."

A few days later, I was staying in his room sleeping on the big chair beside him at the hospice house.

I woke up from dozing. I think it was around 2 a.m. All of a sudden I felt as if my inner being was in turmoil. I started weeping and holding my stomach as I went into travail. It was as if something was tearing away

139

from me on the inside. I cried and cried and then wailed quite loudly. I knew I needed to just let it go. I remember thinking, "what will the nurses think!" I was hoping they weren't alarmed by such a loud noise, and at the same time I knew in my inner man that it was a very sacred moment. It was as if something was ripping apart inside me. After several minutes went by and I let it flow out, all of a sudden it was as if there was a tremendous calm inside me. It was over. Whatever that was, it was finished. As I lay there in that big chair, I heard the voice of the Spirit inside me say, "the covenant is finished."

"What did that mean, Lord?" I quizzed my Heavenly Father. Then it came to me. There was Bear beside me in his hospice bed. He had decided to go to Heaven and we knew he only had a few days left on earth. What is it that ends a covenant? Death. And it was just about to come. The Lord spoke to me that the covenant of marriage with Bear was ended and the ripping apart was the separating of two souls that had become one flesh. I never heard of that before. I've never heard of anyone teach on that. But I knew it was true. I knew I was being separated from Bear and it had happened in the spirit before it happened in the flesh.

Chapter 42
On to Heaven

**In righteousness you shall be established; You shall
be far from oppression, for you shall not fear; And
from terror, for it shall not come near you**

Isaiah 54:14 (NKJV)

Months before Bear wanted to go to Heaven, the
church had planned to send several of our leaders
to the *Operation Explosion Outreach Training*, at Randy
and Paula White's Without Walls International Church
in Tampa, Florida. I was also scheduled to go. We all
had our plane tickets and motel reservations several
months in advance.

I didn't want to go now that Bear was in hospice and
saying he was going to Heaven soon. Bear insisted
that I go.

"You *have* to go," he told me with a serious look on
his face. "Promise me you'll go."

I cried as I told him I couldn't leave him. "Please
don't make me go!" I sobbed.

But after a few minutes I could hear his heart.

"I'll be gone when you get back," he said. "I want it
that way. You have to go and get under the anointing to
carry the ministry to a new level after I'm gone," Bear
was looking at me with those stern Cherokee eyes of his.

It was one of the hardest things I have ever done.

"Alright," I said. "I promise I'll go."

Two days later, I was at the hospice house telling Bear my last goodbyes. My plane was leaving in an hour and a half for Tampa. It would be the last time I would see him here in this life. We said our goodbyes both knowing what was to come. My mind flashed back to the years we'd been together, the victories we'd shared and now the pain we had to endure. I had to go…Bear saw me start to waver. With one last hug and kiss, I was out the door, heading to the airport.

As I rode the plane that day, I could feel the presence of the Lord in an extra special way. I knew I was right in the middle of God's will. As I stared out the airplane window, my mind tried to wander and think about how I would handle everything after Bear was gone. I dozed off for awhile and before I knew it, we were landing at the Tampa airport.

The conference was going well. Randy and Paula knew Bear was about to go home. Pastor Randy had called and talked to Bear before I left for Tampa. They were well aware of the situation and held me up in prayer the whole week I was there.

During the meeting on Wednesday night, I got a call on a cell phone that was handed to me as I sat near the front of the auditorium. I slipped out of the meeting and went to the foyer so I could hear the phone. It was from the hospice nurse. She said Bear wanted to go home to Heaven and would it be alright with me if they gave him the pain shot that he wanted. They said if they gave it to him, he probably would never wake up. That was something Bear always said he wanted, to go to Heaven in his sleep. I told the nurse to do whatever Bear wanted.

I made my way back into the sanctuary and felt like I was going to faint. I asked the Lord to hold me up as my legs felt like rubber. When the meeting was over that night, I went up and told Randy and Paula what the phone call was about. They prayed over me and asked the congregation to join them and stand with me for strength.

The next day was Thursday, September 25th. I called the hospice house and they said Bear was sleeping peacefully and hadn't moved since the night before.

Friday arrived and I was scheduled to go back to the airport around 5 o'clock. I attended all of the meetings I could before my flight. Just as I was ready to leave the motel, the phone rang. It was the hospice nurse. She let me know that Bear had left earth at 4:30 that afternoon, about 30 minutes before they called. Bear got his wish. He wanted to be gone by the time I got back to Fort Worth. It was September 26th and Bear had finally made it to Heaven.

Chapter 43
Rosh Hashanah

To everything there is a season, and a time to every purpose under the Heaven.
                                                    Ecclesiastes 3:1

I flew into Texas that night and headed home. It seemed like an extra long trip, but the peace of God was strong. The next day Pastor George called and invited me to come to that night's special meeting they were having at Eagle Mountain Church. I knew I should go and get around people that would be a support system for me. I was doing well, but I wanted to stay strong. When I got to the meeting, Pastor George made sure I sat by them. Others came up to me to express their love and concern.

Billye Brim was introduced and brought to the platform to speak that night. Her message was all about Heaven, the New Jerusalem or City of Lights. It made so much more sense now as I heard her message and thought about the things Bear said about the music he heard and the lights he saw. I was very comforted as she spoke. I thought about her speaking of the place where Bear lived now.

At the end of her sermon and after the altar call, Pastor George called me up to the platform. My son, Ty and his wife, Rachel were there also, and Pastor George invited any other family members up, so they joined me.

He wanted to have Billye pray over us. Billye didn't know that Bear passed away until she heard it right then.

"So, Bear went to Heaven yesterday? What time?" she asked.

"Yes," I answered. "It was around 4:30 in the afternoon. Billye's eyes lit up.

"Do you know what that means?" She sounded excited. "Yesterday was the Jewish old year ending and the new year beginning. It's called *Rosh Hashanah*. 4:30 in the afternoon was the fourth watch. How wonderful that Bear went home yesterday during the fourth watch! It's a well known fact in Jewish history that only the most righteous people of God go home on that day, at that time!"

Now I knew why it took Bear longer than he thought it would to go home. *God's timing was perfect.*

Chapter 44
I Don't Want to be a Widow!

Pure religion and undefiled before God and the Father is this, To visit the fatherless and widows in their affliction, and to keep himself unspotted from the world.

James 1:27

Soon after Bear went to Heaven, I received a call from the funeral parlor and had to go get Bear's things. Bear's desire was to be cremated, with Ellson Bennett helping to spread his ashes in the mountains of Monument Valley, Arizona.

Ellson and the Navajo people were part of our family. Even though Bear's heritage was Cherokee, this Navajo brother and Bear had a strong covenant. I finally arrived at the crematory and sat out in the parking lot to gain my composure.

I shouldn't have gone alone, but I did. It was hard seeing his watch, his wedding ring and speaking to the funeral man by myself. I started feeling light headed and my eyesight was blurry. I felt as if I were walking in a bad dream and surely I would wake up anytime.

The people were very nice, but I left shaking and in tears. I had never been in that situation before so it was harder than I thought it would be. Unfortunately, ministry is a lonely place at times and sometimes it seems easier to do something by oneself, so I was in the habit of carrying the load on my own. This was one time I was wishing I would have found someone to help walk beside me.

"Jesus, I need you. Carry me," I cried as I sat in my van in the parking lot of the crematory. At that moment, I felt as if no one knew or cared what I was going through, except Jesus Himself. As I sat in the van and cried, the Prince of Peace came and filled that van. Peace literally means, *nothing missing and nothing broken.* I spoke to the Lord right then.

"Daddy," I said through my tears. "You said we would have nothing missing and nothing broken. Well, my husband is missing, my daughter's daddy is missing and my heart is broken." I sat there as if I was in my Daddy's lap, crying on His shoulder. As I shared my heart with Him, He held me in His love and even in what seemed to be my darkest hour, I knew in my inner man that my Heavenly Daddy did indeed have a plan.

When I got home, our house seemed dreadfully empty. There were all of Bear's things everywhere I looked. The phone would ring and my heart would leap thinking it was Bear. A Harley would rumble by and I would look out the window, thinking it was Bear coming home. I would stand at the window, stunned and numb that I really no longer had a man by my side. I received some information in the mailbox that day about being a widow.

"Now that you're a widow," the brochure stated. It said that widow means *empty* and that was what I would be from now on.

"I don't want to be empty, Lord! You have to fill me now," I spoke with my heart aching.

The word widow in the original Hebrew means *forsaken, discarded or desolate.* In the Greek text it means *deficient or lacking.* I knew God would keep His promise and make sure to supply all of my needs according to His riches in glory by Christ Jesus. The Anointed One would surely be my all.

A good brother in the Lord called and said he would come and help me clean Bear's closet and store his things. We worked all afternoon, deciding who to give things to, what to save and what to keep. It wasn't easy seeing all of Bear's things as each one had a special memory attached to it.

Chapter 45
The Memorial

A good name is better than precious ointment; and
the day of death than the day of one's birth.

Ecclesiastes 7:1

Everyone rallied around me to help get ready for the
memorial. There was much to do to get the word
out to the world about Bear's home going, and then
his special day of memory. The date was set for the
morning of Saturday, October 23, 2003. It was just one
month since Bear had gone home to Heaven.

The special service was to be held at Eagle Mountain
Church north of Fort Worth, home of Kenneth Copeland
Ministries. Brother Copeland was going to do the sermon during the service. Pastor George Pearsons was
going to lead the entire ceremony. I was to share some
special words and bring people of my choice up to let
them share what Bear's life meant to them.

While Bear was still at the hospice house, he sat up
in his bed and shared with me what he wanted at his
memorial.

"I want everyone to feel like they're at a party," He
explained. "I just want them to have a happy time and
have everyone served banana splits and root beer floats
at the end of the memorial."

151

I knew I had to trust God for the supplies to get that much ice cream, root beer and bananas. Several people made calls, one put an ad in a local newspaper and nothing seemed to be happening to bring in the ice cream, bananas and root beer. But just like usual, God came through and met every need just in time.

It was finally the day of the memorial. Many friends and family members had come from around the country. We put Bear's bike, a '97 Harley Davidson Fat Boy with his testimony painted on it, in the foyer of the church, along with many of his favorite things. His vest with his colors was at the altar in the sanctuary, along with a huge framed picture of him and one of his favorite Bibles. Next to his Bible was a notebook cover an inmate made Bear as a gift for his Ten Year Anniversary of Freedom celebration I had in his honor in 2001. The leather notebook cover had Bear's release date stamped on it — October 14, 1991, and also stating his Department of Corrections number *627531* was retired.

The church looked beautiful that Saturday morning and everything was in place. Friends began coming in from all over the United States. People from all walks of life; tattoos and piercings, Harleys and leathers to suits and ties were filing into the foyer, lining up to sign the guestbook before they made their way to be seated in the sanctuary. I recognized bikers from several outlaw clubs and many from Christian clubs. All had great things to say about Bear as they greeted me and commented on his example of faith and love while he was on earth. Hundreds of people were walking in from the parking lot as the musicians were taking their place on the platform. Our family members and close friends were all seated in the front row to one side. I gazed around the room at the nearly one thousand people in attendance. I felt an inner strength that only God could put in me as the service was ready to begin. I knew it was a peace that passed all understanding. I was dwelling in the secret place of the Most High for sure.

The band did an awesome job in playing music and leading praise and worship. Pastor George was walking the service out in a completely anointed way as he directed each event in the way it was to take place. Ellson Bennett, our Navajo brother, shared his heart with tears. He then called up Kyle Taylor, a native Pawnee brother to dance in his full ceremonial dress and do the sacred Honor Dance. Kyle shared what it meant before he danced and that it speaks that "Bear did good in life." It was a very holy time as the Native American music played.

Tom Bee, also a Native American brother, sang the song, *Sacred Warrior* in honor of Bear's life. Others shared testimonies as I asked some of our Eagle's Rest people and friends of Loving Hearts to come up and share. It was a very special time as everyone spoke of how their life was touched and changed because of the life lived by the man named Bear Morgan.

Then it was time for Bear's memorial video to be shown. Our friend, Dennis O'Neill had taken a video camera in and captured Bear's heart as Bear spent his last days in the hospice house. *He had taped three different settings — one he spoke especially to the people, one to Micah and one for me.* Dennis had added the last photos we had of Bear — of him at home in his big living room chair by his favorite window with Micah and myself. It made a very appropriate ending to the video. It was a touching time to see him on the big screen and hear his voice, just as if he were really there with us. Bear shared that he wanted us all to know he was excited about going to Heaven, but he expected us all to carry on the work for the Lord.

"Don't be sad! I'll see you all again someday!" Bear smiled as he looked into the camera. "I'll be waiting for you!" he finished as many wiped the tears from their eyes. It was a solemn time even though a strong sense of peace filled the sanctuary anyway.

Bear had a plaque made for Micah without anyone knowing about it. It was a beautiful marble piece with the words inscribed,

> *Dreams do come true*
> *Continue to Dream*
> *Micah Faith Morgan*
> *Love, Dad.*

We had no idea it was being made until the trophy shop called me a week before the memorial. It was a gift Bear had planned to leave his ten year old little girl. It was something she would be able to hold dear to her heart for the rest of her life.

Toward the end of the memorial, I called her up and presented the surprise gift to her. It was a precious blessing she treasures very dear to her heart and is a constant reminder in her bed-

Micah and Dove at Bear's Memorial Service

room of her daddy's love for her and to dream on no matter what is happening around her.

Brother Copeland shared some stories about Bear and then preached a timely sermon on the Covenant of God. The anointing was strong as he finished with the altar call and asked if anyone wanted to give their hearts to the Lord. Several came up for prayer. The entire memorial had lasted around three hours and not a soul moved during the duration of the meeting. Everyone was completely captivated until it was over.

Pastor George closed the memorial inviting everyone to the KCM cafeteria for banana splits and root beer floats as Bear wished. Many stayed for the closing party.

Volunteers were in the cafeteria serving the biggest, best banana splits anyone could have ordered anywhere. The root beer floats were made with the best ingredients, just like Bear wanted it. The fellowship time in the cafeteria was sweet as friends and new acquaintances visited and enjoyed their time together.

Bear's faith always stretched to the limits and got what he believed for and this was no exception. The entire memorial had gone just as Bear requested. It was a time that those in attendance would never forget.

Chapter 46
Spreading the Ashes

And God shall wipe away all tears from their eyes; and there shall be no more death, neither sorrow, nor crying, neither shall there be any more pain: for the former things are passed away.

Revelation 21:4

A few days after the memorial at Eagle Mountain Church, Philip Day, Lain and I drove to Kayenta, Arizona to spread Bear's ashes and to attend another memorial in Bear's honor. Since the Navajo people had taken Bear, Micah and I into their family, Ellson's church wanted to hold a memorial for Bear on the reservation. It was a very special time as Ellson shared some highlights of Bear's life as a covenant brother. Ellson then called me up and honored me with a Chief Joseph blanket, with the turtle pattern. He shared before the congregation that I was part of the family and if I ever needed anything, they would be there for me as a people. As they placed the wool blanket around my shoulders, I felt as if the Holy Spirit Himself was being wrapped around me, comforting me and bringing peace. It was a sacred time that was sealed in my heart forever.

Bear wanted Ellson to help with his ashes ceremony and that his ashes be spread across Monument Valley, one of Bear's favorite places on earth. So the day after we arrived, we all headed out to Monument Valley, on the Arizona/Utah border. Also joining us was our friends Gary and Lu Nelson that were from Mesa, Arizona. We all drove out as far as we could get on a dirt road next to the Mitten Buttes, and parked our vehicles. As we stood below the Buttes, I noticed how bright the sun was shining and how vivid the scenery was even on such a somber day. Gary played the flute to a Native American tune. We all hiked out a little further, and then Ellson took the ashes, held them to the sky and began to spread them to the wind.

All of a sudden, just as Ellson lifted the urn, the wind picked up in a tremendous way. It was as if the Spirit was taking the ashes much farther than we could spread them ourselves. Every time Ellson lifted the urn to spread the ashes, they would not fall down to the ground, but would blow everywhere into the distance. It was a solemn time as we all watched and the flute played. The more Ellson lifted the urn, the more the wind blew. By the time the urn was empty, a huge wind storm had picked up. As we drove back to Kayenta, the storm grew fierce. We could hardly see in front of the vehicle. It was the worse dust storm I had ever seen. We had to head back to Fort Worth that same day and could barely see well enough to drive. The wind had picked up profusely and it was as if Bear was going around the globe once again.

Ellson Bennett spreading Bear's ashes to the wind in Monument Valley.

Chapter 47
Bear's Life Continues On In You

Don't forget about those in prison. Suffer with them as though you were there yourself....

Hebrews 13:3 (NLT)

Now as I write this last chapter, nearly three years have come and gone since Bear's "graduation" to Heaven. God has brought Micah and I a new daddy and husband, Roland Osborne. Roland and I met after Bear's death through his magazine, *Christian Motorsports Illustrated*. He was doing feature articles on "Biker Preachers" and an article on me was submitted to him by *Covenant Woman Ministries* in Fort Worth. I had never met Roland before, but Bear had at one of the motorcycle rallies. It was that article in his magazine that introduced us to each other and the rest is history.

Bear stated before he went to Heaven that the Lord told him his life story would bring more people to salvation after his death than it did during his life. I couldn't see how that could be true until now. Roland is a publisher, writer and editor and has helped me publish a new magazine called *Prison Victory* that goes into the prisons of the world. Every issue is founded on Bear's story with Bear's heart and tenacity, declaring, "You Can Make It When You Get Out." Through the published page, Bear's life story is traveling to more places than he could have ever gone himself. The ministry continues on even though the man has gone to Heaven. One of the greatest honors of any minister is that their ministry would continue even in their absence.

I must say, it has been a real challenge to know what to do sometimes as a wife and mother. How do I carry Bear's story, keep the ministry going, and still honor the new man God brought me?

A few months after Roland and I married, I was really struggling with how much to promote Bear. After all, I was married again, and had a whole new life in front of me. I wanted to honor my new husband and be his helpmeet. It felt like I was married to two men.

"Lord, this is hard. And I know it's not easy for Roland to always hear about Bear." Roland was so supportive, it was as if God had given him a supernatural ability to continue to carry Bear's dream. He NEVER discouraged me from sharing Bear's stories.

One night after I had been struggling with these thoughts, I had a very vivid dream. I dreamed that I was on a huge platform…it reminded me of a Mike Barber meeting in a prison, where there were a sea of inmates' faces looking at me as I brought the Word. I was standing there preaching with all the fervor I had, when I looked down and *out of my belly or my being, came Bear like he was diving off a diving board.* Now, you'd have to see Bear dive into a swimming pool to know what that looked like. He loved to do "belly flops" and splash everyone he possibly could around the pool. So as I looked down at my stomach, there came Bear. He was in his swimming trunks, tattoos all showing and he dove right out of me, into the sea of inmates. I watched him as he made a huge splash as the inmates turned into water and the water went everywhere. Then I woke up. My heart was pounding as I sat up in bed.

Immediately, the Spirit of God shared with me that I was to always preach about Bear's life. Bear's life would always go out to the inmates and make a huge splash, that would have a ripple effect around the world, and change lives forever! Wow, that was the answer I needed. And I've never hesitated to share any of Bear's stories since that day.

I am so blessed to have Roland walking beside me in the destiny that God has set before us. Micah is now 13 years old and Roland is a great daddy to her, too. She has a love for horses so Roland made sure we have a home in the country. Micah has

Micah, Roland, and Dove

been showing her horses and has qualified at state level two years in a row. We are very proud of the young woman she has become. She has also traveled to Costa Rica and to South Africa on mission trips just since Roland has been with us. It took a big man to carry on Bear's family, vision and life story. God found that big man in Roland Osborne. Now together, we're doing just what Bear dreamed of, even before he was ever released from prison back in 1991; that is taking the Gospel of Jesus Christ to the world and setting the captives free.

Bear's life continues on in every man or woman that decides to receive Jesus as their personal Savior and Lord. Bear's life continues on in every man or woman that decides to not ever do drugs or alcohol again. Bear's life continues on in every man or woman that decides they'll never do another night in jail or prison again and then does whatever it takes to stay out after their release. Bear's life continues on in every man or woman that decides to walk away from racial hate and love even those that hate them. Bear's life continues on in every man or woman that decides to forgive even those that did them wrong. Bear's life continues on in every man or woman that declares the Word of God and obeys what God tells them to do.

Accept the *Bear Challenge*. Be one of those that Bear can count on to carry his life on, as he carried on the life of Jesus. *Say the prayer below, today, and mean it in your heart:*

"Father, I come to you in the Name of Jesus. I commit my life to You today in a fresh way. Forgive me for all my sins. I ask You to cleanse my heart, and make me a new person in You. I believe that You are the Son of God and that You died on the cross for me. Jesus, I want to thank You for loving me enough to die for me on the cross, and I receive You as my Savior and Lord right now. Holy Spirit guide and direct me and teach me all the things I need to know. Give me the boldness to walk like Bear Morgan walked and be a godly example for You right where I am.

In Jesus Name, Amen."

When you see Bear again in Heaven, be sure to tell him "thanks." As you have read this book, I know your heart was touched and you have made some adjustments in your own life. You can tell Bear, "Thank you for giving to the Lord. I was a life that was changed."

Let us know you have accepted the

BEAR CHALLENGE

Mail us your name and address to:
P.O. Box 928, Bristow, OK 74010
or e-mail us your name and address:
bearchallenge@lovingheartsministry.org
We'll send you a certificate as a reminder of your commitment.

Chapter 48
Memories from Friends

Mike Warnke,

Celebrations of Hope, Harrodsburg, Kentucky

Susan and I have been in Northern Ireland over the weekend doing a retreat for some friends. We have had a wonderful time and are now on our way to Wales. Today is an "in-between" day.

The rain is "soft." It's a bit cool, but the birds are still singing in the hedges. The clouds roll back and forth across the sky, like sheep out for a romp. In short, perfect Irish weather. It's a day for thinking, writing and naps. It's the kind of day that often makes me think of Bear.

Richard "Bear" Morgan was that rarest of all things; a true friend. There were no strings attached to him. He was, "What you see is what you get." If he liked you, he liked you. If he didn't, he didn't. And you never had to wonder which was which. I liked that about him. It can be a lot of work trying to figure out where people are coming from. It was good to have a friend where there was never a question. Thick or thin, rain or shine — Bear was Bear.

I remember the first time Bear came to the United Kingdom with Susan and me. Having been in "the joint" for all those years, there were a lot of things he had never seen or experienced. It was a "gas" to be there as he looked around all those new corners and over all the unexpected hills. It was almost as much fun watching Bear discover people as it was watching people discover him.

Mike Warnke with Dove and Bear.

Bear was a presence. Standing over six feet tall, with tattoos and muscles all over the place, he was hard to miss. Add the black leather, long hair and the face that mirrored every year he had spent behind bars and you begin to get the picture. The smile was the thing, though. It changed him from a grizzly to a teddy in the twinkling of an eye. It was what drew people to him. Bear never met a stranger and no one else had ever met a bear like this Bear.

It didn't matter if we where on the London "tube," standing in front of Buckingham Palace or just walking down the street. Everything fascinated Bear and everyone was fascinated with him. It never seemed to vary. There was the look of shock as folk became aware of this mammoth moving in their direction. Then came the look of apprehension as they remembered every biker movie they had ever seen. Then there would be eye contact and the smile would sort of burst out all over Bear's face and a new friend would be instantaneously added to the list. No matter who we ran into — kids, grannies, policemen, shop girls; you name it. They all became Bear fans and all it took was one smile.

One of the best memories I have of Bear happened on a day when we were in Wales. We went to visit a famous Bible college near Swansea. The school had been started by the great intercessor Reese Howells and was still in operation long after the great man's death. There were no students present at the time and the only people that were there were two elderly ladies that invited us in for tea. We were taken into a Welsh parlour that hadn't changed much since the early part of the twentieth century. We were all seated on small, embroidered, antique chairs and handed a fine china tea cup with saucer and a matching plate containing tiny cakes and cookies which they call "biscuits." The linen napkins and the sterling silver cutlery and tea service rounded out the picture of a time long past. Bear was in Heaven and so were our hostesses. Picture two diminutive, eighty year old, Welsh ladies dressed in flowered frocks from sixty years ago, with hair of white, sparkling eyes and rosy cheeks. They hovered on each side of this huge biker.

"Would you care for more tea, Mister Bear?"

"Please, enjoy another cake, if you will, Brother Bear."

All of this taking place while John G. Lake and Reese Howells looked down on us from formal portraits mounted on the walls. It was priceless. Bear absolutely loved it! He loved the room. He loved the cakes and tea. But most of all, he LOVED those two ladies. I don't think he had ever had that much grand mothering, all at once, in his whole life. It still brings a grin to my face, even after all this time.

We went on from there. We ministered together over the next week or so. There were many other "Bear moments" along the way. Like when he got tired of what was going on in a meeting and just disappeared. We found him outside leading a bunch of street kids to the Lord. Then there was the afternoon that we lost him again and found him lawn bowling with a bunch of white clad sixty-somethings. He even went off one night to be with Dr. Jerry Savelle in a near-by city.

It was a wonderful trip. Only one of many times Susan and I were able to share time, love and ministry with Bear and his family. I talked with Bear on the day before he passed away. He knew that his time was near. He asked me what I wanted him to do for me when he got to Heaven. I told him to cut us out a couple of Harleys and we would have a nice long ride when I showed up.

"I'll do that, brother," Bear replied. "I'll meet ya' just inside the eastern gate with a Fatboy and a Road King." I'm looking forward to that.

His ministry went behind prison walls and down dark alleys into the bad neighborhoods to find the lost that no one else was looking for. He was a good man. His life started as a disaster and became a testimony that changes the future of thousands of men and women. I miss him very much. Never more than on days like today.

• • •

Flip Lacy, American Airlines pilot
Frederick, Maryland

I met Bear and Dove Morgan on an American Airlines flight from Dallas, Texas to Seattle, Washington. I was flying a trip with a good brother in the Lord, Mark Secrist. Mark was the Captain and I was his First Officer on the MD-80 aircraft. Our flight to Seattle had been canceled and we were booked to "deadhead" (ride in the back) on the next flight to Seattle, to pick up the remainder of our trip. We got seats next to each other near the back of the plane.

Once at cruise altitude, after the Captain turned off the seatbelt sign, I noticed a big, barrel chested, guy making his way to the back of the plane. He had long black hair, tattoos covering his arms and hands, and wearing

a black t-shirt with a picture of a Harley Davidson
on it. I thought to myself,
"Boy I'd hate to meet this
guy in a dark alley!" (Ob-
viously I didn't have the
gift of discernment!) As
he got closer, I noticed
some writing under the
picture of the Harley. It

Bear with Flip and Jeanie.

was a verse from Isaiah 61. We had something in com-
mon! When he was about to walk by, I caught his atten-
tion and told him I liked his t-shirt. We struck up a conversation that lasted for an hour and a half. I learned that
he and his wife, Dove, were going to the funeral of a
cousin that had committed suicide. After the flight was
over we prayed together in the terminal.

It was a match made in Heaven and was the start of
a lifelong friendship and a special bond in the spirit.
God also put it on my heart to partner with them in their
ministry.

Over the years Bear and Dove came to visit us several times and spoke at the church I attended in Frederick, Maryland. They shared their testimony and what
God was doing with the Loving Hearts Ministries. I
never knew Bear before he was saved, but the man I
knew was like no other. He was 100% sold out for Jesus and lived each day for the Kingdom. He challenged
me then and his faithfulness still challenges me today to
make a difference with my life. He and Dove are "spiritual heroes" to me and many others. I say that to
honor them and God's work through them.

It's really neat how God blesses His children. About
a year before Bear crossed over, I was a Captain on the
MD-80 and flying a trip from Washington, DC through

Dallas/Ft Worth, Texas and going on to Tampa, Florida. On the flight to Tampa, a flight attendant passed me a note from Bear and Dove riding in the back. My heart leaped and after the flight we connected and it was really sweet. What is interesting is that I had just talked to Bear on the phone the night before! What a small world.

The next spring they came to visit the Pennsylvania/Maryland area. Bear had been diagnosed with an inoperable brain tumor. My wife, Jeanie, and I were invited to a dinner along with Bear and Dove hosted by some special friends, Gregg and Karen Brady. We had no idea how important that night was in the Kingdom. The dinner was fabulous and the fellowship sweet. After dinner, we went into the living room for prayer and ministry. The time together was really special. Towards the end of the evening something happened that was unscripted, but clearly of the Lord. Bear wanted to pray for Dove. As Bear laid his hands on her and prayed, he blessed her and clearly imparted his "mantle" to her and transferred his authority to her to continue the ministry. We were all taken back a bit, because at that time we all thought Bear was getting better, continuing to walk out his healing. But God's timing was perfect as always!

We attended Bear's memorial service that fall. What a testimony to God's goodness and His faithfulness. It was an event that was to honor someone of *royalty*. I am not idolizing Bear in any way. It's just that we recognized how great a man of God he was and how he lived his life fully for the Kingdom. I again was deeply touched and challenged to live more faithfully and make my life count for eternal values. Thank You Father God for allowing me to be a friend and brother to Bear. As Dove continues the ministry, Jeanie and I are committed to help water the seeds that they sowed.

• • •

Bill Laird,
Hurst, Texas

I met Bear Morgan while I was on the Board of Directors of Mike Barber Ministries in Houston, Texas in early 1992. At the time that I met Bear, my first wife of 34 years had just gone home to be with the Lord, April 29, 1991 and I was still like a baby, trying to learn to walk again. In order to keep myself busy, I became more involved with the prison ministry that I had been working with since 1988.

Bear joined us at a Weekend of Excitement with Mike Barber at the Tucker unit in Arkansas, having just gotten out of prison himself in October of 1991. We were back in the open population of the prison ministering to the inmates when I observed Bear with an inmate. He had the guy penned against the wall with one hand at his throat and the other fist in the air. Very quietly, Bear asked him, "Do you want Jesus or do you want me?" The guy said "Uh, Jesus?" I pulled Bear aside and told him that we can't do that. We must let them choose who they will serve. Bear was used to doing things differently while he was in prison. He said "OK, no problem, I can do that."

Later in 1992, I was asked by Bear and Dove to be on the Board of Directors of Loving Hearts Ministries. Then when my new wife and I were married in December 1995, Darlene became a Board member as well. We have been with Bear and Dove through all the trials and the blessings since that time. These two people had more than their share of opportunities to give up, but never did; thanks to God's love and favor.

Bear always called me to help them make decisions concerning the ministry. One day he called with excitement in his voice. He said, "There are some people who want to give us a tent for our prison ministry and it seats 1,200 people." I asked Bear if there were any strings attached. (The ministry was doing well at the time). He said, "Well, yeah — they do want to join our ministry and become a part of our staff."

I said, "Bear that's too much tent, you don't need anyone to come in and run your ministry. It is your vision; God gave it to you and Dove. Others, though they have good intentions, can cause you to lose focus." Bear said, "OK, I understand that." We didn't take the tent.

Someone came by and offered to give Bear a motor home. They always needed a motor home for the traveling they were doing, so this sounded pretty good. Bear called me and told me that this motor home had low mileage, it was very clean and well kept and the people wanted to just give it to the ministry. All we would have to do is pay off the balance, get our own insurance and oh yes, the people would like to use it every summer for their vacation. We didn't take the motor home.

Bear went to California with the Mike Barber Prison Ministry team to minister to several youth prisons. After a Week of Excitement they left California with the four trucks in a convoy, heading home to Texas. Bear had eaten something that didn't set well on his stomach. Each vehicle was equipped with two-way radios and every few miles, for a while, Bear would tell the others on the two-way that he needed to stop for a restroom break.

After about five stops, one of the workers answered Bear's request to stop on the radio with "Bear we're going to have to get you some diapers at the next stop so we can get on home." There was no response on the radio.

When the convoy got to the 7/11, everyone went in. Bear went and picked up a package of diapers, walked up to the one who made the comment on the radio, shoved the diapers in his belly and said "You wanna put one on me?" Then Bear turned and walked out the door, out to the highway and began walking toward Texas. It took awhile for them to talk Bear into getting back in the truck. Needless to say, the little guy that had made the comment to Bear was very quiet the rest of the trip.

It was Sunday night when the team got to Mike Barber Ministries warehouse in Texas from California. Bear had taken his motorcycle to California in one of the trucks so he was heading home and decided to come by my house on the way. It was about 11:30 pm when he knocked on my door. He came in and sat down at the table and began his conversation with, "Bill, I'm tired of not having food, clothing and things my family needs. I can't even pay my rent. Everything we get we give away. We never have enough to keep anything for ourselves. I could go back on the streets tonight and have $10,000 by morning. I know how to do that, but I don't know how to do this *Trusting God* stuff." He continued, "I think what I'll do is sell my motorcycle that Jerry Savelle gave me. I can get about $18,000 for it. That would get us out of debt."

I said, "Bear, you told me that God gave you that motorcycle for your ministry."

He said, "Yeah, He really did." I said "Well, then if you sell it what else do you have that you can sell after that money runs out? Because if you are going to take over that part of your ministry — finances (and God will let you) — then you need to have some more stuff to sell. Isn't that the way the world does it, Bear?"

We prayed over all their needs and Bear went home. The next day Bear called and told me that he had gone that morning to the post office in Decatur and got a check for $1600 and then to the P.O. Box in Crowley and got another check for $1100. This paid the bills, bought food and other needed things. This being a Monday morning meant that these checks were in the mail boxes the whole time Bear and I were visiting at my house on Sunday night. God already had everything covered. We just didn't know it.

There were numerous times that Bear and Dove would leave home on the motorcycle with seventy-five cents in their pocket to go halfway across the United States to minister to needy people who they knew would not be able to give them any money for the trip. God never failed to meet their needs and they usually had more money when they arrived at their destination than they had when they left home. What a God we serve.

One day while I was working, Bear called me at the office and said "Bill, I'm going to call Kenneth Copeland and tell him we need some help." I said "Bear, that's not the way it works. We have to tell God and let *Him* tell Kenneth or whomever *He* wants to bless for obeying Him. *Our trust must be in God*, not Kenneth. I assure you that Kenneth would rather hear about it from God than from you because he loves to obey God. When you call Kenneth, let it be to give him a praise report about God meeting your needs." Bear always knew the answer before he called me, but he needed to hear it and be encouraged by hearing it.

I have never seen any family live with so many needs of their own and still help meet the needs of so many other families. They never kept anything for themselves. All of those they helped would tell you that the feeling they got from Bear and Dove was that there was plenty in their own house and that they had no needs. The truth was, that those they were blessing had more than Bear and Dove did.

Bear and Dove learned that although they were in a ministry to help needy people, it was their responsibility to teach the people to call on and depend on God and not look to them as their source.

I made several trips to the hospice room to talk to Bear before he went to be with the Lord. He had his mind made up, he wanted to go home.

On September 25, I went to the room after they had given him the last pain shot. They told me that he was not going to wake up and that no one was to go in the room. I said I am a Board member and I want to pray over him. I spent about two hours talking to him and God and then left. The next day the Holy Spirit led me to go back for his departure for Glory. I arrived at about 3:45 pm and he left at 4:30 pm. I'm not sure what that was all about, but God does.

I am sure it took some time for Bear to get to see Jesus, because of all of those that thronged him at Heavens Gates to say to him, "Bear, do you remember me? Well, I would not be here if you had not come to me and told me about Jesus. Thank You, Sir!"

I called Dove in Florida and told her that I was privileged to see Bear off.

Thank God for these two people who gave every bit of themselves for the Gospel.

P. S. God never ceases to amaze me. Just look at this new guy, Roland Osborne, that He put in Dove's life to help her continue the ministry. Welcome, Roland, we love you, too. Thank you, Jesus!!!

• • •

Pastor George Pearsons
Eagle Mountain Church, Fort Worth, Texas

Bear Morgan was such a treasure to Terri and me, and to our church. When we first met him after he was released from prison, he was rough around the edges — well, more like "jagged" would better describe

173

Bear. The time had come for him to receive some formal training for ministry. He decided to attend Jerry Savelle's Bible School. The dress code required a suit and tie — of which Bear had never worn in his life. So, off to the store he went along with several of our pastors. It was quite interesting to see him all dressed up, combed hair and starched shirt. He did look a bit uncomfortable, but became acclimated to it after a while. We were all proud of him the day he graduated.

I also remember the time I had to counsel him about some areas of his life that needed to be renewed. We sat down together in the little speaker's room to the side of the sanctuary on a Wednesday evening. I had to speak very bluntly and honestly. He received what I had to say. But he told me later on that the Lord had really helped him that night because he really wanted to punch me for what I said. I'm sure glad the Lord restrained him!

The most important encounter I had with Bear was several days before he departed for Heaven. I was sitting by his bedside. The end — rather the beginning — was near. He began to speak. Instead of bemoaning his own situation, he spoke of all the "little" ministries that needed assistance, encouragement and support. He said, "Don't forget the little guy." He was right. I assured Bear that the Lord would take care of them. That seemed to put him at ease. He was able to lie back in his bed and relax. He was gone within the next two days. That's our Bear — always caring for people, concerned for the lost and wanting to do something to help — right up to the very last minute.

• • •

Kenneth Copeland
Kenneth Copeland Ministries, Fort Worth, Texas

I know a lot of men that could have and would have stood the same test had they been in the same position as Bear. But this is the only man that I ever saw with my own eyes, do what he did. He gave a man, Ellson Bennett his word that he would be in Kayenta, Arizona at the *Healing of the Nations* motorcycle rally. I was speaking there and Bear told me he was going to be there too and preach with me. In the meantime the devil tried to kill him, and almost did. Right before the rally Bear crashed his bike. The doctors had to put his head back on his spine and put him in this terrible looking halo thing bolted to his skull. Even though the doctors wanted him to stay in recovery, Bear said, "No, no, no I have to be in Kayenta." They said you aren't going anywhere hoss. But Bear insisted that he had to keep his word.

The doctors warned him that he would die if he went, and Bear's response was, "That don't matter, if I die then I will die preaching. I am going to that meeting and I will preach with Brother Copeland." My son-in-law flew him to Kayenta while Bear just layed in the back and slept the whole way. Bear went on to preach, broken neck or no broken neck. I thought, "Well he gave them his word, so he had to be there."

I saw him do this again, but only this time he was dying. Breathing his last breath, on his death bed, body had shut down, the whole thing. Then all of the sudden Bear starts getting up out of bed. Dove asked him where he was going. He said he was going to the bathroom. Bear then mentioned that he gave Ellson his word to be at the biker rally this year. So instead of dying he kept his word and came to the rally. Now you can say what you want to, but number one, that takes a lot of faith, number two, it takes a lot of man, and number three it takes A LOT OF GOD.

I shared these things to let you know that I am proud to know this man, to be a part of his life, family, and to be in covenant with him. I appreciate him.

• • •

Jerry Savelle
J.S.M.I., Crowley, Texas

One of my fondest memories of Bear was while he and Dove were attending my Bible School in 1995 and the Holy Spirit instructed me to give them my new Heritage Softtail Classic motorcycle.

I had the entire student body go out to the parking lot and there we presented Bear with this beautiful Harley.

Here was this great big man crying tears of joy and it touched each and every one of us.

Bear won a lot of people to Christ through that motorcycle and I have never regretted investing it into his life.

• • •

Todd Powers
J.S.M.I., Crowley, Texas
Powers Ministries International, Thailand

Bear Morgan will always have a special place in my heart. I had the wonderful privilege of being his "Dean" when he attended our two-year Bible College. I have so many amazing memories of Bear that it would almost require a book like this one to tell all the stories.

Bear and Dove attended *JSMI Bible College* about three years after Bear had been released from prison. Needless to say, he was still a bit rough around the edges (not just a bit…we're talkin' *rough*). At that time in his life, he had a real problem with authority. So, as the Dean, I represented authority — something he didn't like or appreciate — and he thought his job was to challenge me, the school, the system and anything else he could find. We required a suit and tie — he wanted to wear jeans and leathers. We required assigned seating — he wanted to sit wherever he wanted. We prohibited cheating on tests — he wanted Dove to do his tests for him. And the list goes on...

One incident stands out to me; we had taken all the students to Houston, Texas to conduct a three day outreach. We had "one of those moments" when Bear refused to do what was being required of all the students. So, I had to confront him and deal with him in a loving, but stern manner. While I was speaking to him, he interrupted me and began to yell in my face as he said in front of all who were standing in the convention center lobby, "take this (his school id card) and shove it up your @!&#*+%!" and then he stormed off. Come to find out later, Bear said that if it were not for all the people standing around, he would have beaten me right there and then. Thank God for those who were there in that lobby that day. Bear would always say of me that I am the smallest man to ever "get in his face" and live to tell about it.

During his time at the Bible school I could see his life changing — thanks to the Word of God, the Holy Spirit and his precious wife Dove. When I would look in Bears eyes, within him I could see a loving, compassionate and tender man. I knew deep down inside there was an awesome person in there. As I lovingly and fearfully earned his respect, Bear and I became friends. He would come into my office and we would talk about God and ministry and life. We would pray together and laugh and cry together. I was amazed as I saw a man's life changing before my eyes. A man who was full of hate began to love. A man who despised black people began to embrace them and love them. A man with no discipline or control began to develop a life of excellence. I'll never forget the time we went to

Bear sharing Jesus in Nairobi, Kenya

Africa together and I witnessed Bear, a man that had been so transformed by the power of God, ministering the love and compassion of God to the blackest African you would ever meet. I knew his life had been changed! I knew by this time that Bear loved me like a brother because whenever anyone tried to *mess with me*, he would *get in their face* and *take care of the situation.*

The day we awarded Bear his diploma from Bible College was a day of great joy and triumph for all of us. Bear and Dove went on to accomplish many great things for the Kingdom of God. They had an amazing anointing to love the unlovely…to lift up those who were down and out and to speak into the lives of people who would never darken the door of a church or listen to a traditional preacher. Everywhere they went in the U.S. and around the world they would love the unlovely, help those who were hurting, proclaim the name of Jesus and absolutely terrorize the devil!

I thank God for Bear, his life and the legacy he has left. Let's learn a lesson from Bear's life and do our best to bring the best out of others.

● ● ●

Happy and Jeanne Caldwell
Agape Church, Little Rock, Arkansas

We were friends with Bear and Dove for many years. We found them to be very delightful people… always "up", with a smile on their face.

Bear was a gentle giant. He always had something good to say to you. They were definitely positive people.

I remember one summer the motor home they traveled in broke down and was towed to our parking lot at Agape Church. It was a challenging time for them, but they walked in faith and soon they were back on the road again.

From time to time, they visited our church and were always a blessing. In fact, Dove ministered at one of my Ladies Bible Studies that I have each month. We all wore motorcycle outfits. It was a time many will never forget.

We will always remember Bear and the strength he portrayed as he walked with the Lord.

●●●

Mac Gober
Canaan Land Ministries, Autaugaville, Alabama

The one thing I noticed more than anything about Bear Morgan was his heart. It was bigger than all of Texas. He was like any man, even me. He went through happy days and through days that sometimes looked discouraging. But he never ever, not one time quit Jesus, and putting other people first. That was Bear and Dove's whole heart, to reach people for Jesus Christ.

I remember when Bear had been in a serious motorcycle accident. It was a miracle that he was not killed immediately. You just have to know the strength of Bear. If you have ever been close to him, you realize how enormous he really is.

Bear and I were scheduled to speak at Kayenta, Arizona. Brother Copeland was holding a three day meeting at the Healing of the Nations with Ellson Bennett. One of Kenneth Copeland's pilots and I flew to pick Bear up. When we landed, I saw Bear coming out to the plane. I didn't realize how serious the accident was until I saw him. It looked like he was wearing a big steel halo with bolts through his neck and head to keep him from moving his head. Kenneth told him that he didn't have to come and speak. He realized Bear's condition was very serious. But Bear wouldn't quit, not even then.

I think Bear slept most of the way to Arizona. When we landed and got out of the plane, you could tell Bear was in pain. He never asked anyone to feel sorry for him. He didn't look to anyone for pity. He was just glad to be there speaking with our good friend, Kenneth Copeland. Most men wouldn't have even thought of doing what Bear did. Bear was just being Bear Morgan. He wanted to reach the people in that Indian nation for Jesus Christ.

That night I saw an awesome miracle take place. Bear laid down his life for the people in that Indian nation. Bear will always be in my heart. Bear and Dove are two of the most incredible people I have ever met. They are totally unselfish always helping others. That's their legacy that will always be remembered.

• • •

Johnny Moffitt
Voice in the Wilderness Prison Ministry, Dallas, Texas

My word for Bear is committed. If Bear was your friend, he was your friend. He and I traded motorcycles one time and he committed to pay me on a handshake. That was during a tough time for him and money was not always available for a payment. But he was committed to his word, and eventually, he paid every cent.

When I had my heart attack in Tennessee, Bear drove all night to be with me and he sat by my bed until after the surgery. He was *committed* to his friends. Once when Bear was scheduled to speak at a COPE (Coalition of Prison Evangelists) conference in Branson, MO, he showed up with a wire brace (halo) on his head. He had driven his bike off of a mountain near Yellowstone and broken his neck. He was *committed* to his commitments. He was my friend and I miss him very much.

• • •

Danny Trichell
D.T. Ministries, Monroe, Louisiana

There is a story in Luke 7 beginning in verse 37 about a woman who came to the Pharisee's house where Jesus was and began weeping and washing his feet. The Pharisee thought to himself, if this man is really a prophet he would know this woman is a great sinner. Jesus knew his thoughts and told the Pharisee about a man who had forgiven a big debt and a little debt. Jesus then asked the Pharisee which one do you think will love the most? In verse 47 it says...he that is forgiven much, loves much.

Every time I read this scripture, I think of Bear. Bear loved people and Bear wanted people to know the love and forgiveness of Jesus more than anything in the world. One time as I was visiting Bear at Loving Hearts, a woman came in suffering from cancer. Bear stopped everything he was doing, laid hands on her and prayed, "Lord, you said that concerning the works of your hands to command you, so in Jesus name I command you to heal this sister." Bear was truly bold in Christ and that woman was healed!

Another great memory is the time Bear came to my hometown and we ministered together to a crowd of four-hundred hardcore inner-city juveniles from a state facility. Because of an emergency our time was cut short. Bear gave a quick message and then I read from Romans 10. That day about 300 young men gave their lives to Jesus. You should have seen the love that man had for those kids. Later, as my future wife and I served Bear a huge vat of gumbo, (the real reason Bear came to Louisiana, ha-ha, Bear *loved to eat*) he tried his best to convince us to let him marry us. I told him that in Louisiana we have a three day waiting period, but he was pretty insistent.

I didn't know Bear before his conversion, but if the love that I saw in this man was any indication of his past, then his life is truly an awesome testimony of the grace of our Father. To whom much is forgiven, he loves much. That was Bear.

• • •

Dennis Burke
Dennis Burke Ministries, Arlington, Texas

There is a small café in Puebla, Mexico that makes the best tacos you have ever eaten. One night in Café Super Salsa, I sat with the host of our convention, Kelvin Box, his wife Monica, Bear, Dove and Micah their daughter as well as two other ministers. We had just finished a full day of ministry and had come to eat and relax together.

Bear and Dove had invited me to come to Puebla to meet Pastor Kelvin as well as to be a keynote speaker of the Walking in Victory convention. It was taking place right in the heart of the city at the convention center. Bear showed his deep passion for the Word as he ministered to these beautiful people in Mexico. The entire week was packed with powerful ministry and many

Bear and Dove ministering in Mexico.

salvations. It was obvious Bear was deeply loved by those wonderful friends in Mexico.

Yet, my memory of that one night at Café Super Salsa remains one of my favorite. As we enjoyed our conversation around the table we continued to eat and order and eat some more. The ladies ate very little, but Bear and I went all out. When we finally finished we realized that we had ordered a total of 48 tacos — and they were all gone!

I continue to go each year to Puebla for the Walking in Victory convention. I also continue to go back to Café Super Salsa with Pastor Kelvin. Each time I enter the small building, smell the cooking and order my tacos, I think of that wonderful night with my friend Bear laughing and loving the good life God had given him.

• • •

Bobby Doran
Born Again while a prisoner at the Eastham Unit, Texas

Not a day passes by that I don't remember Bear and Dove Morgan. It's almost as though my life depended on it. Yes, I know God could have used many other ways to reach me, but he chose to use Bear and Dove — Papa Bear and Mom. For me, they were a bridge to hope. I met them while in administrative segregation in a Texas prison where I spent most of my time. It took a man like Bear Morgan to reach in through the concrete and steel and show me the love of God.

Bear and Dove were obedient to their ministry assignment from Jerry Savelle's Bible School. They were given a list of inmates that needed to hear the Gospel and I was on that list. They wrote me a letter and told me about the love of Jesus. I wrote back to them and cussed them out; telling them to take their God and leave me alone. But then I thanked them for the letter anyway since I hadn't had any mail for a long time.

I thought I was just a throw away from the system and the world had no use for me. I had used up all my chances. But I didn't know God loved me. Then they came to visit me in person. Bear brought the Spirit of the Lord with him when he reached into my cell. We were alike and I knew that his change was real. He was a different kind of preacher. He was real. God knew I needed something real. God knew I had shut the door on many others who weren't, so He knew which man to send me — Bear Morgan. He was a man's man, a lover of God and his family. He was the only man to ever tell me he loved me. It penetrated my heart and soul.

In 1995 I made Jesus the Lord of my life and was called into the ministry. I may have been in prison, but the prison was no longer in me. Like my spiritual father, Bear, I was commissioned by the Lord to continue sharing the Love of God that passes our understanding and passes through the concrete and steel in our lives, physically, spiritually and emotionally. I got out in 1998 after being locked up for nearly 17 years. Bear and Dove accepted me as I was and brought me up as their own. They endeavored to instill in me the truth from God's Word. I am ever thankful for the times we spent together. I love you Papa Bear and Mom.

● ● ●

Ellson Bennett
Covenant of Faith Ministries, Tempe, Arizona

Bear Morgan showed me what a true brother is. He also taught me what a real covenant is. What I remember about Bear the most is that he was a man of integrity and of his word.

One time he was in the hospital from a broken neck and he was scheduled to speak at the Healing of the Nations meetings that I was hosting in Kayenta, Arizona. He made them release him from the hospital early just so he could keep his word to me. Brother Copeland flew him in to the meetings and he preached the night he got there — halo and all. Bear showed everyone what a warrior really is.

• • •

Allen Shook
Pastor of Freedom Church, Burleson, Texas

Words cannot describe the man that Bear Morgan was. A giant in the spirit world and an overcomer in action for many to see.

Being on the mission field with Bear was life changing for everyone who met him. The war was going on and bullets were flying everywhere. None of us were confident that we were leaving Albania. Because of Bear's faith

Bear with Pastor in Albania.

and warrior mentality, he brought such courage to the team. Courage was the thing that I noticed most about Bear. He knew HIS GOD and he knew that he had been in worse places and God always came through for him. The people of Albania still talk about Bear Morgan. His love touched many.

When he was in my class in Bible School, I saw his hunger to know God and up until the end, he still had that hunger.

●●●

Wayne Bredahl
President, Righteous Riders Chapter,
Circuit Riders Motorcyle Ministry, Prescott, Wisconsin

I grew to love Bear more and more as the years went by. Bear and Dove would come up each year to go with us on our bike run to the Great Lakes and each year I could see more of Jesus is his eyes. Eyes are a window to our soul and I could see the awesome changes that God was making in his life.

I watched Bear play with my sons, Adam and Josh, and I could tell that he loved them very much. I could also see that Bear was enjoying the childhood that he never had, while he was playing with my boys. It was like he was taking back what the devil had stolen from him.

I remember one time when my son Adam was struggling. Bear asked how Adam was doing so I shared with Bear what was going on. Bear hadn't had much sleep that week, but he said he would wait up for Adam to come home because God showed him something in a vision. Well, Adam didn't come home until 2 a.m. and Bear met him at the door and loved on my son in those early morning hours. That was like Bear; to do whatever it took to share the love of Jesus to everyone he was in contact with.

I never knew the old Bear, but I knew and loved the new Bear. He had buried the old Bear and lived the new life in Jesus Christ.

●●●

Philip Day
Biker brother, Fort Worth, Texas

Bear was a true brother. In fact, he told everyone I was his real brother and everyone believed it since we were the same size. They believed whatever Bear said since they didn't want to argue with him.

Philip and Bear

What I remember most about Bear was that he was a man of his word. If he said he would do something, you could take it to the bank that it would get done. He even went all the way to South Dakota to rescue one of the men from the men's home.

I miss my Bubba very much.

Other Resources from Loving Hearts Ministry

BEAR'S Testimony — Outlaw Biker, Captain of Arian Brotherhood and notorious killer... You'll be totally touched when you hear the life changing transformation that Jesus Christ wrought in MAD DOG Morgan's life after he gave his heart and life to Christ.. Audio CD $6 + $4 S & H

— SOON TO BE RELEASED —

You Can Make It When You Get Out — Bear's own book that he wrote to help you get out and stay out. He passionately believed in the saving grace of Jesus Christ and the empowerment of the Holy Spirit to make right choices in a person's life. Hear God's heart through Bear and his passion for those captives that will be set free when they read this book.

Hatch That Dream — Dove's call is to facilitate the fulfillment of other's dreams. One of her most challenging success stories is the worldwide eternity-changing ministry of Loving Hearts with Bear Morgan before his death. In *Hatch That Dream* she shares her heart, her wisdom and her hard fought experiences. The Holy Spirit will anoint you to move into your own destiny as you read this book.